COLORING YOUR BRAND

DOPRESS BOOKS

CYPI PRESS

PREFACE

Color is something that provokes an emotional response. We often react to color long before we notice anything else about a brand or a product. Color speaks to us in many ways, and in making our choices of color we are, consciously or subconsciously, making a statement; however, more often color chooses us. We all have favorite colors; perhaps they bring to mind exotic places, visited or imagined, or a simple nostalgia of candy wrappers and other childhood memories.

Color is also extremely powerful. When walking in central London and seeing the slightest glimpse in the distance of a yellow bag — immediately I know it's Selfridge's. I don't have to see the name; the color is completely synonymous with that brand. The same can be said for a number of other brands: Tiffany and blue, Cadbury and purple. Brand designers know this, and they use it, to a very good effect. This book is a brilliant study of colors in the design landscape, colors that belong with brands, or simply "are" brands, helping us navigate through modern life with ease. Green, yellow, blue, orange, or simple color blocks represent many things or combinations that inspire and intrigue: luxury, simplicity, freshness, and adventure. Pink and orange represent doughnuts or rather, "donuts;" brown equals some of the best luggage money can buy.

I am often asked to name my favorite color — and I keep coming back, throughout my 20 years in design, to Pantone 810, which is a fluorescent yellow. It always brings a smile to my face.

Michael C. Place

Michael's career spans three decades, beginning in 1990 when he left his studies to pursue his dream of designing record sleeves. In 2001 he founded Build, a contemporary design studio, producing modern graphic design solutions for independent and corporate clients.

Michael, featured in the 2007 film "Helvetica — A Documentary Film," has spoken at numerous conferences worldwide and has several times been a judge at the prestigious D&AD global awards.

CONTENTS

RED

IJUP 2012	008
Hotel Lone	010
William Prescott	012
The Inside	014
Unit	016
BPA	018
Katona József Theatre	020
Arthography	022
Harajuku Gyoza	024
826 Baltimore	025
Ariadna Haberdashery	026
Oswald Publishing	028

ORANGE

Maison Théâtre	030
Bloom Branding Consultants & Designers	032
Beunit	034
Smartson	035
Paper Moon	036
Orange Hive	038
ING Direct Spain	039
Faust	040
Rebranding Teachers	042
Kosan Gas	044

BROWN

Penny Royal Films	046
ACASA	047
One Trick Pony's Alcoholidays	048
Poncelet Cheese Bar	050
Magnum Temptation	052
Caballo Viejo South American Whiskey	054
Palomino Restaurant	056
Bömarzo	058
Avant Garde	059
Incessant™	060
Beans	062
Justin Horacek	064
Lee — Never Wasted Bag	065
Nördik Impakt 13	066
Adam & Eve Law Firm	068
Choose Your Beef, Brand Your Cow! — The Cow Boy	070
Jeopardy Magazine	071
Sas & Lance's Wedding	072
Primera Fila	074
Schuck Juwelier	076
Celebrating Marriage	078
Golden Racket	080

YELLOW

SJ Options	082
Lingua Viva	084
Nankin Lab	086
Motozone	088
Kino Klub Split	089
Dumoulin Bicyclettes	090
Teacake Stationery	092
Terralec	093

GREEN

Uptown966	094
Lime Wharf	095
HOLT	096
Elena Hannover	098
projectGRAPHICS	099
Yelloblue	100
Future Fortified	102
Comma	104
Metronet	106
Menorca	108
Dear Me Brasserie	110
Tim Muldowney Painting	112
AM1000 Studio	113

CYAN

Petrol Handmade Accessories	114
Montreux Cafe	116
Mr. & Mrs. Mehlhoff's Wedding Invitation	117
Nerbo	118
3E Architecture	120
Hunchworks	121
frameLOGIC	122
Empowering Performance	124
Vintage and Cofee for Music	125
The Greenwich Hotel	126
Officeria	127

BLUE

NH Vínculos Comerciales	128
Odooproject	129
Lisn Music	130
The Peak Lab.	132
Café du Monde	134
Tobogán	136
Mannaz	137
Samsung Developers	138
Naturally Different	140
InsureRisk	142
Vadim Zadorozhny's Vehicle Museum	143
Literary Tea	144
Lucky Brand	146
Baltic	147
Going Donuts	148

PURPLE

Lamon Luther	152
Onkja	153
Confeitaria Lopes	154
T & Cake	156
The Collection	158
Megabox	160
Bespoke Tailoring	162
The Flower Company	164
Doner Kebab	165
Sandra's Haarschnitt	166
Art Fabrica	167

MAGENTA

Monkey with Guns	168
Artspace	170
Flor Aguilar's Personal Identity	172
Econcern	173
Jazzy Innovations	174
Sladunitsa	176

MULTICOLORS

International Game Days	178
Anoniwa Corporate Stationary	180
Soul Kitchen	181
Piccino	182
Yoshida Design	183
Dilly Dally	184
Rítmia Music Therapy	186
Storyline	188
Vrrb Interactive	190
Brighton Road Studios	191
Waldo Trommler Paints	192
Le Bilboquet Laurier	194
Bumsies	195
Marawa — The Amazing	196
Chocolat Factory	198
Victoria Harley	200
Camping de Dalt	202
Frederik Lindstrøm	203
Glad Creative	204
Lakomi	205
Maurer	206

GREY

TIN CAN	208
The Great Courses	210
John Casablanca's International Institute	212
MEDNUT — Tigernut Orxata	214

BLACK

Noeeko ID	216
Box Cafe	218
AG	220
Ravens Heaven	222
Hyde Park Brewery	224
Lise Madore	225
Hörst	226
MORE Bike Park	228
Rock the Vote	230
The Danish String Quartet	232
Belmacz	233
Black Cow Vodka	234
Brass Developments	235
Grebban Design AB	236
Work & Play	238
Bërthama	239
Gargalo	240
Knucklehead Musik	241
Local 360	242
Nikolaj Kunsthal	244
Hugo	248
Moloobhoy & Brown	250
Artisme	251
Concrete Business Cards	252

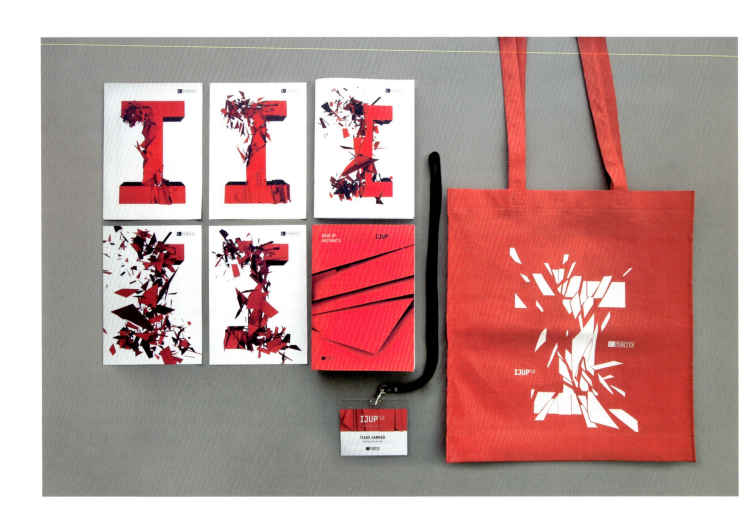

IJUP 2012

Year of Completion_ 2012
Designer_ Tiago Campeã
Photography_ Tiago Campeã
Client_ University of Porto

IJUP is an event created by University of Porto to promote young researchers and research done among undergraduate and graduate students. To catch young students' attention to the event, the idea of creating a distinctive and bold identity, closer to a more irreverent and direct speech, resulted in an "exploding I" (short for Individual, Information, Investigation and IJUP), which illustrates the boom of information, inherent to any research process, as well as the explosion of knowledge implied in the sharing environment of the event.

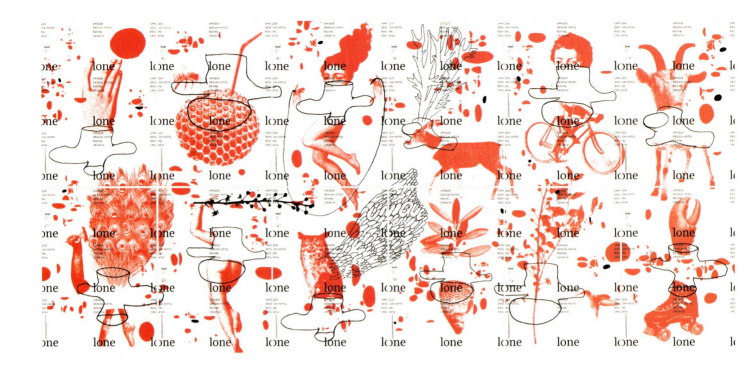

Hotel Lone

Year of Completion_ 2011
Design Firm_ Bruketa&Žinić OM
Photography_ Domagoj Kunic
Client_ Maistra

Hotel Lone is a showcase of Croatia's creative industry, with several of the nation's best architects, designers, and artists involved in its creation. Bruketa&Žinić OM is in charge of the hotel's visual identity. The key visual is inspired by the central lobby, which is the most impressive space of the hotel, extending along its entire height. All the important applications are part of a large 4-meter illustration created based on the visual identity. When combined, they create an integral image.

William Prescott

Year of Completion_ 2012
Designer_ Piotr Steckiewicz

This is the branding for imaginary fellow William Prescott. At first it was supposed to be a branding redesign for a lawyer with the same initials, but eventually the designer and client parted ways. The designer decided to finish the project anyway, and really had a lot of fun with the freedom of creating without constraint. The designer changed the original colors, name, and industry.

The Inside

Year of Completion_ 2012
Design Firm_ Alexandra Turban
Photography_ Alexandra Turban
Client_ The Inside

"The Inside" is an international fast food restaurant that specializes in pocketed goodness: baked, fried or boiled foods, according to the traditional recipes of distant lands, or new extravagant taste creations. The features of these "pockets" are the super hot content, and the natural inner values of the food inside the pockets. These features are not only the inspiration for the restaurant name, but are also reflected in the graphic style. The simple, minimalist illustrations play with the concepts of "inside" and "inner values."

C3 M100 Y100 K1

C23 M38 Y47 K0

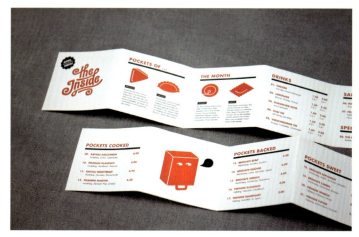

Unit

Year of Completion_ 2012
Design Firm_ Emanuele Cecini
Photography_ Daniel Sax
Client_ Emanuele Cecini

This is an art direction project for a mechanical engineering company based in NYC. The client's main objective was to express their expertise with a strong and modern corporate brand. The identity, using solid red and a very geometric sans serif typeface, communicates their goal-driven and solution-centered attitude.

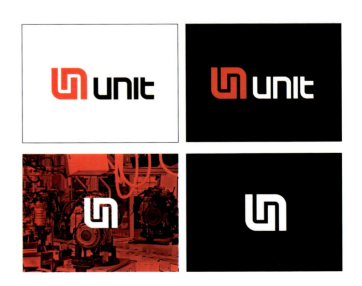

BPA

Year of Completion_ 2012
Designer_ Ingeborg Scheffers
Photography_ Dirk Wolf
Client_ BPA

For this firm of contractors, a corporate identity has been developed based on one form, the logo. When repeated, the logo has an effect similar to the tape used to cordon off an area under construction. Eight business cards together form a ribbon that can be accordion-folded into a booklet. A single business card can be torn off when needed.

Katona József Theatre

Year of Completion_ 2012
Designer_ Botond Vörös
Photography_ Botond Vörös
Client_ Katona József Theatre

The negative space in the quote mark refers to a well-known motif—theatre masks. The designer has chosen a very intense color—red—next to black. Red is commonly associated with danger, sacrifice, passion, beauty, blood and anger, attributes which are necessary for a good theatrical performance.

C10 M100 Y100 K0

Font

AaBb Cc123
PF Din Text Cond

PF Din Text Cond Bold
ABCDEFGHIJKLMNOPQRSTUVWXYZ
abcdefghijklmnopqrstuvwxyz
1234567890
ÁáÉéÍíÓóÖöŐőÚú

PF Din Text Cond Medium
ABCDEFGHIJKLMNOPQRSTUVWXYZ
abcdefghijklmnopqrstuvwxyz
1234567890
ÁáÉéÍíÓóÖöŐőÚú

PF Din Text Cond Light
ABCDEFGHIJKLMNOPQRSTUVWXYZ
abcdefghijklmnopqrstuvwxyz
1234567890
ÁáÉéÍíÓóÖöŐőÚú

Colour

Pantone DS 77
100%

CMYK Black
100%

Sign

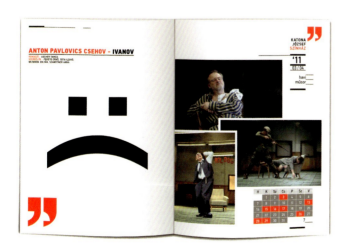
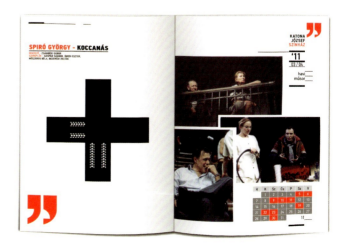

Arthography

Year of Completion_ 2012
Design Firm_ Arthography
Photography_ Dmitry Shentyapin
Client_ Arthography Studio

An austere, type-faced logo is supplemented by a concise symbol that is used in all printed materials. Designers preferred unusual materials rather than standard chalk overlay paper. Seals of different colors are attached to scarlet and black envelopes made of textured paper. Promotional leaflets with business cards are enclosed in the envelopes.

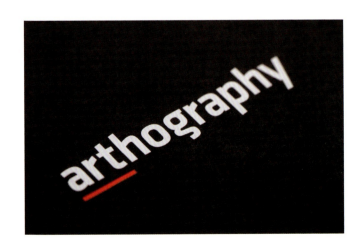

C14 M98 Y100 K4

C0 M0 Y0 K100

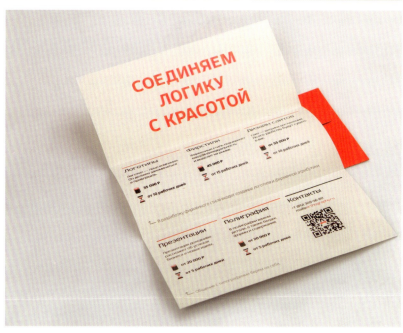

C21 M97 Y91 K12

Harajuku Gyoza

Year of Completion_ 2012
Designer_ Alan Crowne
Photography_ Jesse Smith
Client_ Harajuku Gyoza

Harajuku Gyoza is a new restaurant recently opened in Australia. The theme was inspired by Japanese gyoza restaurants, featuring pan-fried dumplings found in the Harajuku street culture in Tokyo. The brand needed to be iconic and memorable. The designer wanted to pull together both the charm of the Harajuku style and the clean interior design of Japanese gyoza restaurants. He began with the identity by developing a Harajuku-inspired gyoza character as a focal point for the brand. This alone was enough to create the personality.

826 Baltimore

Year of Completion_ 2009
Designer_ Stefanie Horodko
Photography_ Stefanie Horodko
Client_ Personal Work

The design for this corporate identity system was based on the 826 National brand. The designer was given the random location of Baltimore, and, through research, came up with a unique 826 store in that area. This location is home to the renowned Johns Hopkins Hospital and University, so this Doctor Store is to identify with that specific area. The designer researched apothecary artifacts and aimed to reference the style of that era in an updated, modern way through illustration and typography.

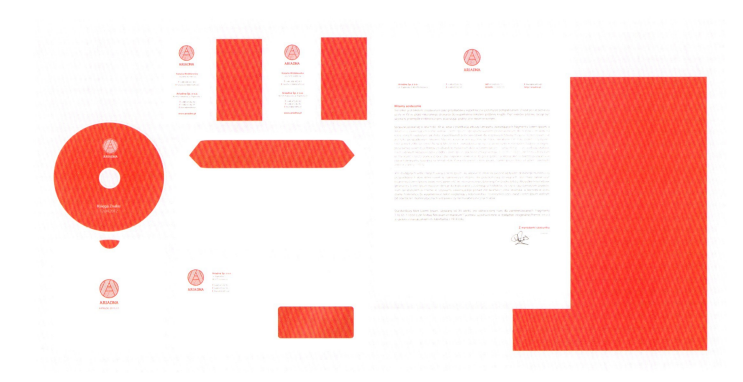

Ariadna Haberdashery

Year of Completion_ 2012
Designer_ Alicja Wydmanska
Photography_ Alicja Wydmanska
Client_ University Project

A new corporate identity concept for Ariadna S.A. Thread Factory from Poland was the subject for this project. The project was created specially for Higher School of Art and Design in Lodz. The logo connects the letter A (from the brand name) with a skein of wool. Both the symbol and the type are tightly designed, pure geometric forms. The use of the color red makes the design fresh and feminine.

Oswald Publishing

Year of Completion_ 2012
Design Firm_ QJS Design Studio
Photography_ QJS Design Studio
Client_ Oswald Publishing

This is the new identity designed to embody Oswald publications' ever-changing audience and to create a timeless yet unique design sensibility, which juxtaposes modernity, simplicity, and powerfulness. The color scheme is the eye-catching red, which makes the identity vivid and concise. These give consumers a feeling of efficiency and resoluteness.

C8 M90 Y85 K1

C45 M81 Y72 K66

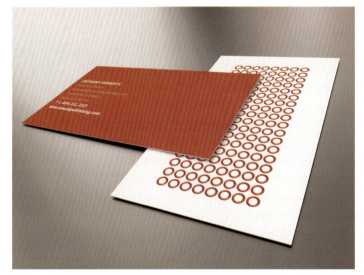

Maison Théâtre

Year of Completion_ 2007
Design Firm_ lg2boutique
Client_ Maison Théâtre

The Maison Théâtre is a distributor specialized in theatre for the young public. It's also an association of 27 creative theatre companies for youth. Maison Théâtre naturally turned to lg2 to update their branding. This new branding enables the Maison Théâtre to carve out a leading position in the world of cultural entertainment for families with an identity that clearly evokes its mission: to put on plays developed and produced by professionals, for a public between two and 17 years old.

C0 M88 Y84 K0

C22 M100 Y78 K15

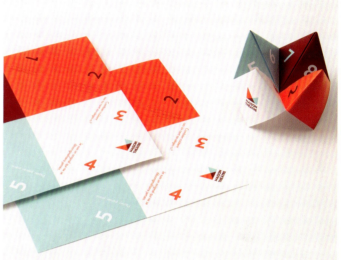

Bloom Branding Consultants & Designers

Year of Completion_ 2012
Design Firm_ Bloom Branding Consultants & Designers
Photography_ David López Herrero
Client_ Bloom Branding Consultants & Designers

Bloom is an independent brand design agency with locations in both Saudi Arabia and Spain. For its logo and branding, designers decided to replace the second letter "O" with a circular arabesque element, which was in turn designed to evoke a diverse range of shapes and suggestions: a flower, a heart, the "B" of "Bloom," or a fountain; viewers can imagine their own symbolism. This Spanish-Arab creative nexus aims to represent a modern, albeit corporate "convivencia" in the fields of graphic design and visual communication.

C0 M85 Y85 K0

C0 M0 Y0 K100

Bloom Corporate typeface
Avenir LT

Branding

Ø$%&@ A1&'

LOREM IPSUM DOLOR SIT AMET

SEDEGET
VELITNIBH
SCELERISQUE
SEDURNA
ANTELIA
VENENATIS
ULTRICIES
ALIQUET
SEDLEO
NULLAM

PRETIUM
MAGNA
VOLUTPAT
RHONCUS
CONSEQUAT
PULVINAR
INTERDUM
DIGNISSIM
EGETTELLUS
SUSCIPIT

Beunit

Year of Completion_ 2013
Design Firm_ Kreujemy.to, Piotr Ploch
Photography_ Kreujemy.to
Client_ Beunit

Beunit is a Saudi Arabian computer programming company that is interested in developing social media such as websites and mobile apps. They strive to serve society by facilitating connection in better ways. The design team decided to create an abstract sign that could be a reflection of unity and programming. They came up with the idea of two different shapes that combine together creating a letter B. The whole sign has a high-tech feeling, which represents its goals and works perfectly for the company.

Smartson

Year of Completion_ 2012
Design Firm_ Brandoctor
Photography_ Igor Manasteriotti
Client_ MMM Agramservis d.o.o.

Smartson is the biggest smartphone center in Croatia. Brandoctor created the brand from scratch; their sister agency Brigada designed and branded the retail space. The brand idea was inspired by the street-smart approach of the owners. This is embodied in the name Smartson, the slogan "Be smart," and the visual identity of a friendly, useful "smart guy." The retail space followed the brand guidelines, turning out to be a modern, warm, and inviting place.

Paper Moon

Year of Completion_ 2012
Design Firm_ Catherine Renee Dimalla
Photography_ Catherine Renee Dimalla
Client_ Personal Project

Paper Moon is a self-authored 1940s' style dim sum restaurant and lounge in the spirit of historical Chinatown. A traditional Chinese banner is the source inspiration for an illustrative logo that transforms to a tag-like business card. The cards feature a persimmon red front and a patterned back, complete with hand foiling for a more accessible alternative to letterpress. The day menu is a hanging lantern, while the evening menu takes a more traditional format with a rich tassel that references the logo.

Orange Hive

Year of Completion_ 2012
Design Firm_ Emanuele Cecini
Photography_ Daniel Sax
Client_ Orange Hive

This work showcases the branding project for a new creative agency based in Frankfurt. This includes a logo design, stationery, website design, and the art direction for the photography. Emanuele's highly detailed approach delivered an end product that was very much in keeping with the German design studio's own internal design philosophy. The branding is straightforward and uses a limited number of elements and information: In the logo one finds a surprising and elegant balance of lines and empty spaces; the pop of color provided by the orange accents gives the ensemble a nice twist, preventing it from being boring, and presenting instead the clean and classy minimalism it achieved.

ING Direct Spain

Year of Completion_ 2012
Design Firm_ Ruiz+Company
Client_ ING Direct Spain

This is a visual identity project for ING Direct Spain. Through the orange color, typography, and an iconic pictogram system created specifically for ING, Ruiz+Company created a graphic code to transmit the brand, its personality and values.

Faust

Year of Completion_ 2011
Design Firm_ Matadog Design
Photography_ Matadog
Design Client_ Faust

Faust is a post-production house based in Athens, Greece. The designers' task was to create the corporate identity of Faust based on their logo. The cat figure was the key element used in building the corporate image. Orange and dark grey were the only colors used. Both sides of the letterhead were printed; the business cards were die cut.

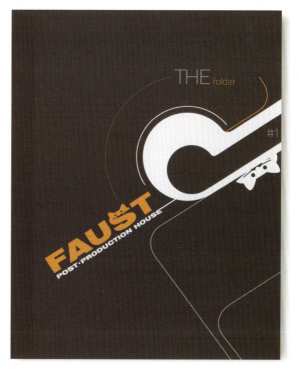

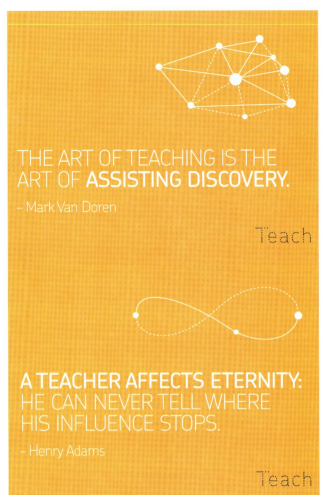

Rebranding Teachers

Year of Completion_ 2012
Design Firm_ Hyperakt
Client_ Studio 360

Teachers are currently represented by uninspiring, childish visual imagery. Images like apples, chalkboards, and the ABCs neither revere the profession of teaching nor do justice to the intellectual and creative development teachers help guide in students of all ages. WNYC's Studio 360 asked Hyperakt to create a new design vocabulary that reflects the multidimensional roles of teachers. The solution is all about connecting the dots: The designers created a boundless visual language that celebrates teachers and the process of developing ideas.

Kosan Gas

Year of Completion_ 2010
Design Firm_ Ineo Designlab
Photography_ Ineo Designlab
Client_ Kosan Gas

Kosan Gas is an old Danish brand within the industry of gas, energy products and services. The logo was inspired by the original Kosan Gas logo from the 1950s. The new logo, combined with a contemporary font with rounded details and a very consistent use of color, creates a unique visual look with both hints of "retro" (used for marketing purposes) and more modern elements (used for basic corporate communication).

Penny Royal Films

Year of Completion_ 2012
Design Firm_ Alphabetical
Photography_ Alphabetical
Client_ Penny Royal Films

As a production company, Penny Royal Films leads the field in animation, visual effects and direction for film, television and web-based graphics. Inspired by the humble penny coin, the designers created a priceless monogram logo in copper foil which appeared at the same size as a penny coin across all applications including business cards, stationery, packaging, marketing announcements, and online graphics.

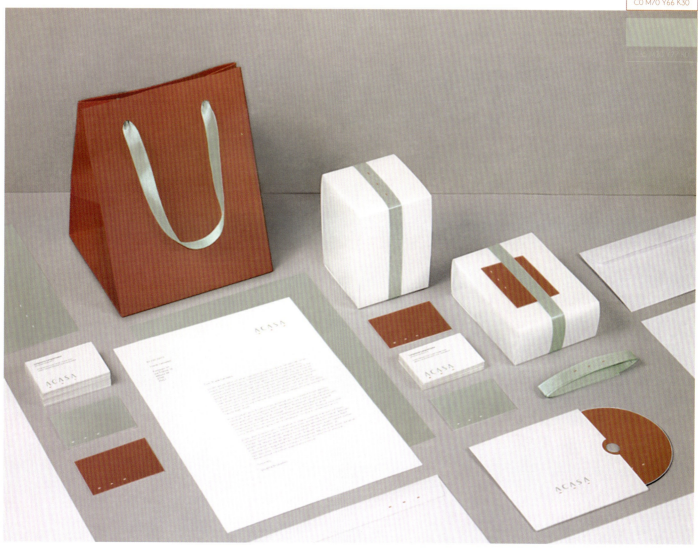

ACASA

Year of Completion_ 2011
Designers_ Augusto Arduini, Giuditta Brusadelli, Gianluca Crudele
Photography_ Augusto Arduini, Giuditta Brusadelli
Client_ Personal Project

ACASA is a branding design proposal for a contest sponsored by Politecnico di Milano. It is a competition for a hotel project. The logo expresses what the word ACASA means. The letter "A," without the horizontal stem, represents home comfort. The graphic rhythm of the logotype transmits balance. The harmony is emphasized by the dashes of the letter "A." With the dashes moved away they whisper the graphic cadence of the letters. Dashes are the core. They are the intense particulars of the house. They are living details.

One Trick Pony's Alcoholidays

Year of Completion_ 2011
Design Firm_ One Trick Pony
Photography_ Mike Mielcarz
Client_ Self Promotion

"Alcoholidays" is One Trick Pony's annual self-promotion celebrating awesome clients and hard work with a little hard liquor. The 2011 Alcoholidays theme was YULE LOGIN. The studio sent out bottles of tequila in hollowed-out wooden logs, complete with custom labels and shot glasses, both made of wood, with graphics and instructions burnt into them.

C40 M90 Y76 K60

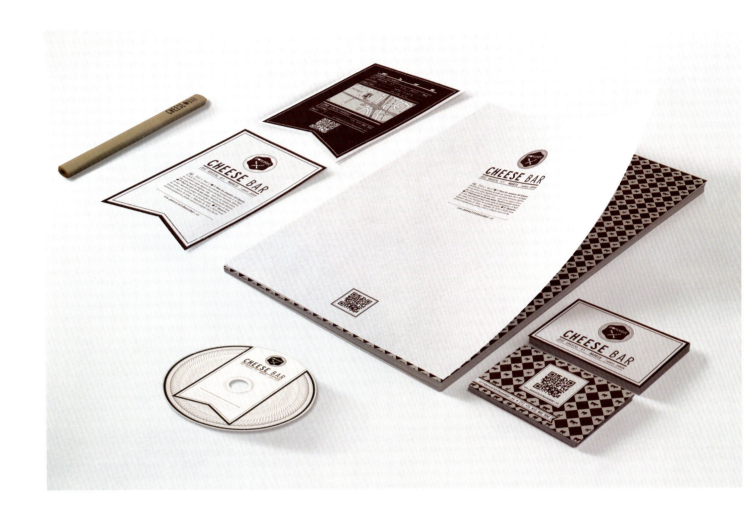

Poncelet Cheese Bar

Year of Completion_ 2011
Design Firm_ Gabriel Corchero Studio
Photography_ Gabriel Corchero Studio
Client_ Poncelet Cheese Bar

The main concept of this project is accompanied by a space and an identity and based on the "care of nature." The details are present throughout the development to create a truly unique space lasting in time. According to the elements revolving around the project, the designers return to the origins and create an innovative and timeless craftwork from a cutting-edge standpoint.

C0 M73 Y100 K80

C35 M50 Y68 K12

Magnum Temptation

Year of Completion_ 2012
Design Firm_ Somewhere Else
Photography_ Somewhere Else
Client_ Mercury M.C.

To launch the new Magnum "Temptation" line of ice cream, a generous marketing kit filled with scented candles, room scent, soap bar, and a series of postcards with famous quotes about temptation were put together. The press kit is presented as a jewelry box, built around the phrase "Resist everything but temptation," with sticker seals that taunt recipients to give in to curiosity. The project features a customized typeface unique to the campaign.

Caballo Viejo South American Whiskey

Year of Completion_ 2012
Designer_ Ruben Jimenez
Photography_ Ruben Jimenez
Client_ Personal Work

Caballo Viejo South American Whiskey is a visual identity system project that consisted of branding a fictional company as if it were real. The project included a logo, stationary set, package design, and a website storyboard. The designer chose to do a whiskey because it represents a high-class liquor and, aside from the liquor packaging itself, the designer could incorporate more accessories like T-shirts, hats, whiskey glasses, key chains, clocks, bag packs, and other collateral material.

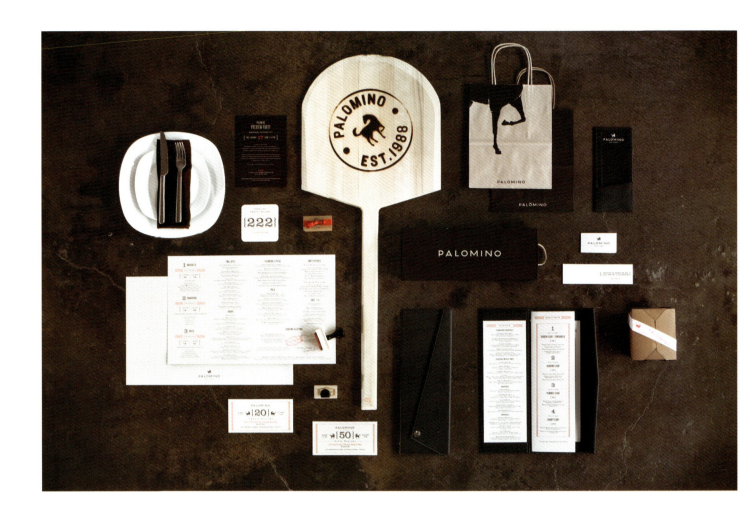

Palomino Restaurant

Year of Completion_ 2011
Design Firm_ Superbig Creative
Photography_ Rina Jordan
Client_ Restaurants Unlimited

Palomino is a small, multi-location restaurant located in key cities across the United States. Being a 20-year-old restaurant, it was due for rebranding. Superbig was given the opportunity to overhaul Palomino's branding across all consumer touch-points, including logo, menus, advertising, and messaging. It was important for them to reflect the vibrancy, heritage, and dedication to quality in Palomino's new identity and maintain consistency in all endeavors.

Bömarzo

Year of Completion_ 2011
Design Firm_ Atipo
Photography_ Atipo
Client_ Bömarzo

Bömarzo is a new coffee and brunch brand. Atipo created a symbol for identity synthesizing the entrance of gardens through the "ö" with dieresis mark that is a character of northern European alphabets. The "ö" symbol evokes the images of their products, subtly delivering the messages.

Avant Garde

Year of Completion_ 2012
Design Firm_ Design Devision
Photography_ Xenia McBell
Client_ Avant Garde Cafe-Resto-Bar

The aim of this project was to create a minimalist contemporary visual identity to co-exist with the historical center of the town in the Greek island of Zakynthos. Inspired by the meaning of the French word "avant garde" as the front line in the army and cutting edge in culture, designers created the symbol of an arrow which points to the top. The background pattern, which denotes a net or waves, was inspired by the sea.

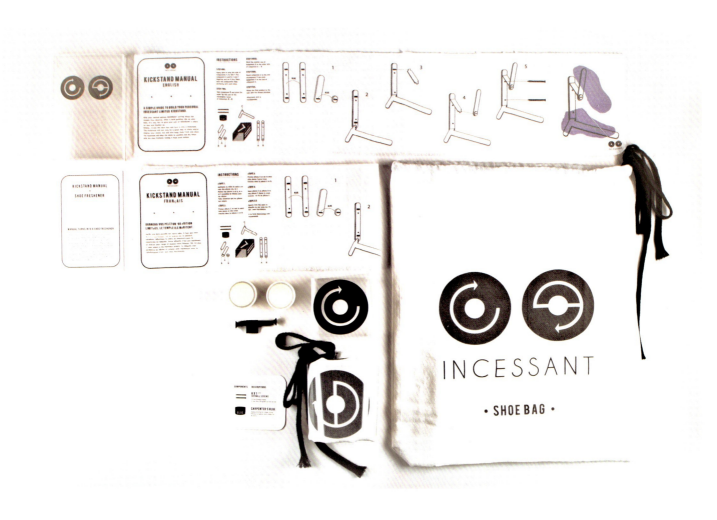

Incessant™

Year of Completion_ 2012
Designer_ Jinah Lee
Photography_ Stephen Han
Client_ Personal Work

The design for Incessant™ shoe packaging meets the following objective: Create an environmentally sustainable shoebox that also creates additional value to the consumers' purchase. It includes a shoe stand, with parts integrated into the shoebox itself to reduce any excessive material consumption, and an instruction manual that can be used as a shoe freshener instead of being thrown out.

Beans

Year of Completion_ 2012
Design Firm_ DRY Creative Projects
Photography_ DRY Creative Projects
Client_ Beans AB

Beans is a Swedish coffee supplier with a strong ambition to serve coffee that both tastes good and is good for the environment. The colors that are used in the design symbolize their core values of having delicious coffee while being "down to earth" and "green."

Justin Horacek

Year of Completion_ 2012
Design Firm_ Berger & Föhr
Photography_ Jamie Kripke, Sam Campbell
Client_ Justin Horacek

Inspired by the graceful shape of the sinusoidal waves that move through the earth, the designer decided to channel their unseen beauty into heirloom-quality furniture. Named after the physicist who determined how to best model these waves, the Fourier stool embodies the qualities of strength, integrity and flow.

Lee — Never Wasted Bag

Year of Completion_ 2012
Design Firm_ Happy Creative Services
Photography_ Happy Creative Services
Client_ Lee

The "Never Wasted Bag" is a shopping bag designed by Happy Creative Services (from India) for Lee, the well-known jeans brand. It can be used and reused in so many ways — as a bookmark, a CD sleeve, a calendar, and in many more ways. This is a really hip and interactive way to promote Lee's image; it is continually positive when people recycle this bag because the Lee brand name stays visible in any way the bag is used.

Nördik Impakt 13

Year of Completion_ 2011
Design Firm_ Murmure Creative Agency
Photography_ Paul Ressencourt, Julien Alirol
Client_ ArtsAttack!

The Nördik Impakt Festival, an evening electronic music event, communicates via limited edition collector goodies. For this occasion, Murmure developed conceptual products around electronic music and phosphorescence, which are supported with two reading levels. The agency made posters and invitation cards that extend the graphic design, and reveal its electronic spirit when the lights go out. The designers unveiled a concept with a totally innovative design by creating the electro-phosphorescent sunglasses made out of paper.

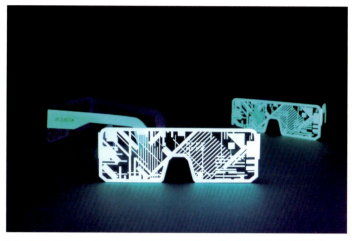

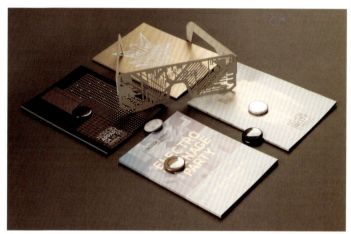

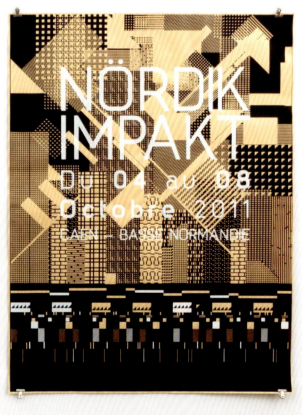

Adam & Eve Law Firm

Year of Completion_ 2011
Designer_ Raewyn Brandon
Photography_ Erin Strong
Client_ Adam & Eve Intellectual Property Law Firm

The challenge for this project was to create a law firm that pushed the creative boundaries of branding and marketing with a slightly controversial approach, using religious influences to drive the design. The concept was to play off God's creation and the Ten Commandments He gave Moses. Traditional Biblical philosophies communicate Adam & Eve's values as an intellectual property law firm. The design direction synthesizes traditional styles with modern techniques.

Choose Your Beef, Brand Your Cow! — The Cow Boy

Year of Completion_ 2012
Designer_ Livia Ritthaler
Photography_ Livia Ritthaler
Client_ Personal Work

"The Cow Boy" was Livia Ritthaler's major project at Middlesex University in London. The concept is a restaurant where people can brand their own cow. They have to gamble with the barman to get a free whiskey and, most importantly, the designer wanted to emphasize where the steak comes from. Natural materials meet minimal design, with the flair of a wild young western.

Jeopardy Magazine

Year of Completion_ 2012
Design Firm_ Catherine Renee Dimalla
Photography_ Catherine Renee Dimalla
Client_ Jeopardy Magazine

Jeopardy Magazine is the literary and fine arts publication of Western Washington University that showcases the unique creative works of the university community each year. The overall feel is that of an apocalyptic tome, with a lattice of Mayan motifs printed with a spot varnish. The varnish shines in the light on a completely matte graphite cover stock. Gold is an important symbolic element for the Mayan culture, as well as among many other civilizations, so gold is an important color element in the design.

Sas & Lance's Wedding

Year of Completion_ 2012
Design Firm_ Sorbet Design
Photography_ Nicole Miller-Wong, Sheahan Huri
Client_ Sas & Lance Donnell

This project is a design of identity, art direction, and website design for the wedding of Sas and Lance Donnell. Rustic beauty and old-fashioned romance were apparent throughout, from the stock and the color palette to the physical map. All were created with the same strong commitment to the visual theme.

C34 M42 Y56 K5

C35 M93 Y79 K51

Primera Fila

Year of Completion_ 2011
Designer_ Núria Pujol Canals
Photography_ Carles Mercader, La Blogothèque, Núria Pujol Canals
Client_ Personal Work

Primera Fila (First Row) is a music collective that offers a new perspective of a concert: Everyone is on the first row, at home. The goal is to enjoy an intimate experience, as the stage barrier disappears. It is presented as a "Do It Yourself" proposal because people experience it at their own homes, in an act closer to a craft concept than to mass consumption. However, that doesn't prevent PF from having a contemporary and fresh identity, appropriate to its audience.

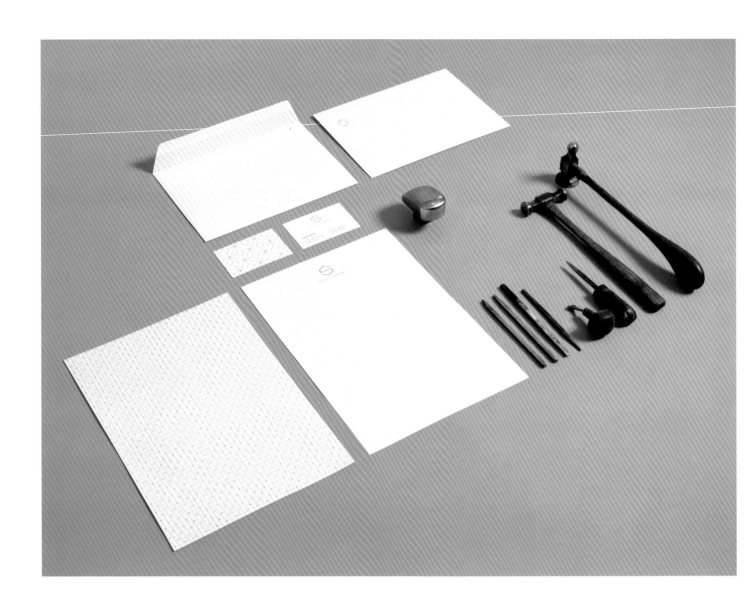

Schuck Juwelier

Year of Completion_ 2011
Design Firm_ Ineo Designlab
Photography_ Ineo Designlab
Client_ Schuck Juwelier

Schuck Juwelier is a high-end jeweler based in Widen, Switzerland. It specializes in designing and producing unique, exclusive jewelry for a wide range of international clients. The identity design is based on the geometrical shapes of diamonds and pearls. The overall expression is kept clean and simple to convey luxury and style.

Celebrating Marriage

Year of Completion_ 2012
Design Firm_ Anoniwa, Naoto Kitaguchi
Photography_ Yuka Yamaguchi
Client_ Non-Commercial Work

It all began with the implementation of personal logos for wedding celebrations. This particular logo was created using a leaf motif, in order to reflect a ball in an old mansion surrounded by greenery. Various forest animals were chosen as the key visuals to give those in attendance an enveloping, warm atmosphere for the special day.

C45 M50 Y100 K0

C0 M0 Y0 K100

079

Golden Racket

Year of Completion_ 2013
Designer_ Maksim Arbuzov
Photography_ Maksim Arbuzov
Client_ Amateur Moscow

The Golden Racket was designed for The Annual Tennis Amateurs Award. The main idea was to create a unique symbol for the Golden Racket, which should combine elegance and modern style. It would not only speak to the tennis community as a whole, but would also work equally well anywhere. The basic shapes that form a racket, the frame and a grip influenced the overall design. A color scheme of gold, teamed with black was dictated by name Golden Racket.

C49 M54 Y100 K40

C0 M0 Y0 K100

SJ Options

Year of Completion_ 2011
Design Firm_ Higher
Photography_ Higher
Client_ SJ Options

SJ Options is an option trading course and mentoring program based on the "Max Safety, Max Reward" option trading strategies. SJ Options' training addresses today's volatile and fast-moving market conditions, and is based on unique and innovative option trading strategies that provide much more safety protection against sudden losses. Higher provided the full circle of branding services, including brand identity and website design.

Lingua Viva

Year of Completion_ 2011
Design Firm_ Necon
Photography_ Necon
Client_ Lingua Viva

Lingua Viva is a well-known language school in Poland. The aim of the rebranding is to adjust the visual identification system of the school to current market requirements. Necon aimed to refresh the image of the company by designing a new logo for the school as well as by designing and launching a brand new website. The process was supplemented with the introduction of a complete set of printed materials to be used in both internal information flow and outdoor advertising.

C2 M25 Y100 K0

C5 M38 Y100 K0

C55 M61 Y68 K49

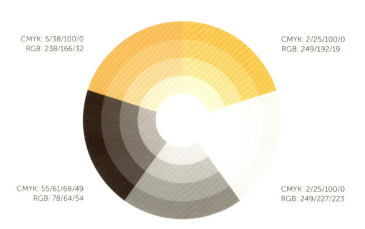

CMYK: 5/38/100/0
RGB: 238/166/32

CMYK: 2/25/100/0
RGB: 249/192/19

CMYK: 55/61/68/49
RGB: 78/64/54

CMYK: 2/25/100/0
RGB: 249/227/223

CMYK: 33/28/34/15
RGB: 153/150/142

Nankin Lab

Year of Completion_ 2012
Designers_ Pau Garcia Sanchez, Pol Trias Coca
Photography_ Pau Garcia Sanchez
Client_ Nankin Lab

There is a rare pleasure in seeing a building collapse, in tearing a piece of paper in half, or in blowing up a balloon. These are acts that last less than a second; being so ephemeral, these acts allow a greater experience in a shorter time. These are situations involving speed and high intensity. Nankin Lab is a design studio that recreates these moments to generate new projects.

C0 M5 Y100 K0

C0 M0 Y0 K100

Motozone

Year of Completion_ 2012
Design Firm_ Thorbjørn Gudnason
Photography_ Thorbjørn Gudnason
Client_ Motozone

Motozone is a firm that specializes in high-end auto parts. The company shies away from discount products and regards serious car enthusiasts as a target market. The Motozone logo works a bit differently than usual: The word after "Moto" changes, depending on the department.

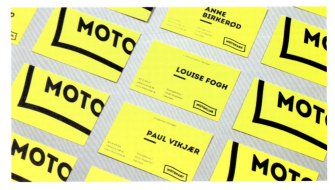

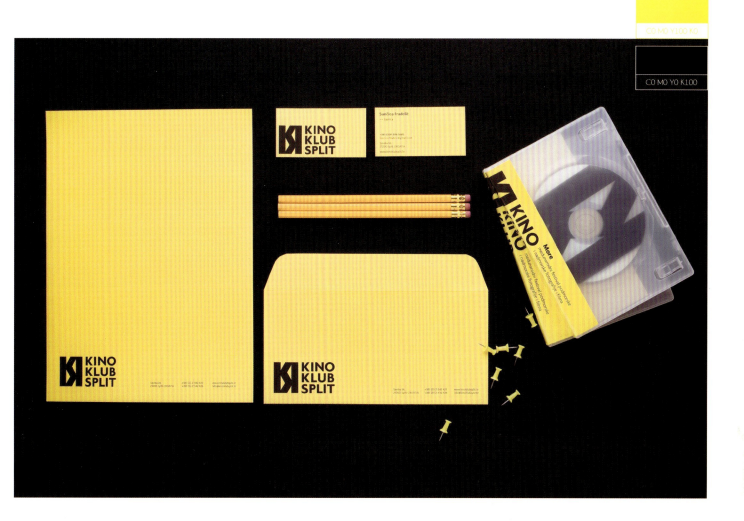

Kino Klub Split

Year of Completion_ 2009
Designer_ Hrvoje Hiršl
Photography_ Hrvoje Hiršl
Client_ Kino Klub Split

Kine Klub Split was founded in 1952 and its work has been recognized by the public as one of the original components in the history of Croatian nonprofessional, alternative, amateur cinematography. The symbol of the logo is constructed from the initials of the name, "Kino Klub Split" — KKS, by connecting two lowercase "k"s, the letter "S" is constructed. The symbol is reminiscent of the film tape. Black and yellow are used since the logo is mostly applied on the filming equipment and visibility is important.

Dumoulin Bicyclettes

Year of Completion_ 2011
Design Firm_ Sébastien Bisson
Photography_ Sébastien Bisson
Client_ Dumoulin Bicyclettes

While moving to a new location, Dumoulin Bicyclettes decided to rethink its corporate branding. More than just a shop, Dumoulin Bicyclettes is an essential place to access and exchange practical and fun information. The design is meant to recall the signage along the bike paths in Montreal. Humorous quotes on the walls, T-shirts, business cards, and cycling maps: All are printed in yellow, black and white. The logo — a capital "D" and a lowercase "b" — are drawn with dotted lines, reproducing the yellow lines seen on the pavement in Montreal.

Teacake Stationery

Year of Completion_ 2011
Design Firm_ Teacake Design
Photography_ Teacake Design, Sebastian Matthes
Client_ Teacake Design

Teacake Design aims to offer forward-thinking ideas; at the heart of their work is the desire to provide innovative solutions, tailored to suit their clients' needs and ambitions for the future. They listen, engage, and work hard to offer an informed insight. Teacake Stationery includes rather splendid business cards and letterheads, printed on Factory Yellow, photographed trendily next to some tools from around the studio that echo the images on the letterhead.

Terralec

Year of Completion_ 2012
Design Firm_ John Barton
Photography_ John Barton
Client_ Terralec

The project is the new identity for stage lighting and equipment supplier Terralec. Full stationary ranged from light-gathering business cards made from fluorescent Perspex, through to lanyards and packaging tape. Letterheads and compliment slips were printed on PopSet Yellow 100gsm. Business cards details were laser cut into 2mm Fluorescent Perspex Yellow.

Uptown966

Year of Completion_ 2011
Design Firm_ WonderEight
Photography_ WonderEight
Client_ AL Mawaed

The client came to WonderEight for help in creating a new concept in a star location in Saudi Arabia. The location used to host a winning concept with a success story in the area, and this was the challenge designers were excited to take: gaining the client's acceptance with expectations already set to "high." Although the offering was the same as the previous concept, they created a completely new experience that leaves people with a familiar feeling at the end of their visit.

Lime Wharf

Year of Completion_ 2012
Design Firm_ FRS London
Photography_ Joseph Turp
Client_ Family Mosaic

This identity scheme subtly references the juxtaposition of the property's contemporary design and the historical use of the canal on which it is located. As the name of the property development was predetermined, the lime green color scheme was an obvious choice. Using dark grey as a secondary color provides a broad tonal range allowing maximum standout for the brand's lime green primary color.

HOLT

Year of Completion_ 2012
Design Firm_ YR Studio
Photography_ Shutterstock
Client_ Holt

Holt is a wood furniture manufacturer, presenting some high-end designs crafted of specially selected, high-quality wood. The concept of branding and identity for Holt was inspired from a wooden chair, which is also the gestalt letter "H," meaning Holt. The shape is more modern and dynamic according to Holt's desired character — friendly and unpretentious.

C38 M11 Y100 K0

Elena Hannover

Year of Completion_ 2012
Design Firm_ +Quespacio, Ana Milena Hernández Palacios
Photography_ David Rodríguez Pastor
Client_ Elena Hannover

Elena Hannover is a conceptual store that offers clothes and accessories for women in the media and high-level occupations. Their audience is the modern trendsetter, between 25 and 40 years old. A corporate identity is created to represent all the primary values of the brand that also are represented in the shop.

C60 M10 Y100 K0

projectGRAPHICS

Year of Completion_ 2010
Design Firm_ projectGRAPHICS
Photography_ projectGRAPHICS
Client_ projectGRAPHICS Studio

The objective for the corporate identity was to create a minimal visual concept and an easy way to produce it, while following the colors and the direction of the logo. The green sticky tape is the main element used in the entire corporate identity. Through this, the designers created a connection between all of the corporate identity materials. To emphasize the symbolism of the green, the designers combined it elegantly with black and white, creating light on the black side and at the same time giving life to the white side.

Yelloblue

Year of Completion_ 2012
Design Firm_ Horizon Draftfcb, Sami Joe Mansour
Photography_ Sami Joe Mansour
Client_ Yelloblue

This project involved the naming of and corporate branding for a company specializing in renewable energy and green solutions in Lebanon. Designers came up with the name Yelloblue, which, combined together, give the color green. The main concept of the identity consisted of a spectrum of fresh colors ranging from yellow to blue, via green, applied boldly in the stationery and branding materials. The designers created a customized type formed of circular shapes representing the earth. The corporate font chosen for the stationery is "VAGRounded," whose rounded edges and smooth shapes are a perfect match for the identity.

Future Fortified

Year of Completion_ 2012
Design Firm_ Apartment One
Client_ GAIN (The Global Alliance for Improved Nutrition)

GAIN is working to end global malnutrition through home fortification packets that provide the essential nutrients for giving birth and raising healthy children. Apartment One developed the creative brand for GAIN's first national campaign. They crafted the brand voice and visuals to be both empowering and accessible. Included in the graphic language is a system of blank white boxes that allows individuals to make their own marks on the campaign — and on the future.

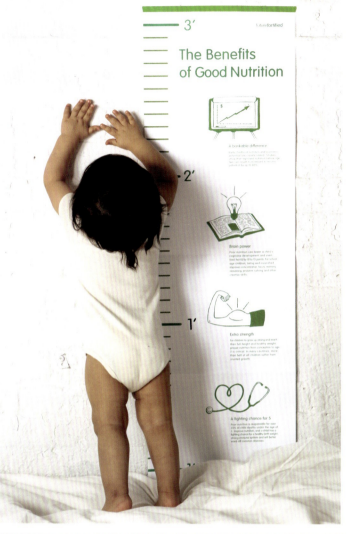

Comma

Year of Completion_ 2012
Designers_ Caroline Rosenkjær, Casper Holden, Christina Stougaard, Nicolai Henriksen, Thorbjørn Gudnason
Photography_ Thorbjørn Gudnason
Client_ Comma

The company wanted the designers to analyze the Scandinavian market, find a target group, design and name the product, create a complete visual identity, and introduce it to the market with a hard-hitting advertising campaign. The concept behind the Comma design is that, just like a regular typographic comma which creates a pause in a sentence, Comma is the break in the pregnancy process when having trouble conceiving. To communicate this visually, the designers replaced the typographic comma in their sentences with the Comma package.

Metronet

Year of Completion_ 2012
Design Firm_ Work in Progress, Torgeir Hjetland
Client_ Metronet

Metronet delivers services within SEO, PPC, development and design, e-commerce, social media, and web analytics to a wide range of clients. The identity reflects the name, its references, and expectations. The color scheme is from DOS and the first computer screens; the type is OCR-B, made to facilitate the optical character recognition operations by specific electronic devices. The illustration for the identity is an abstract global system of interconnected computer networks.

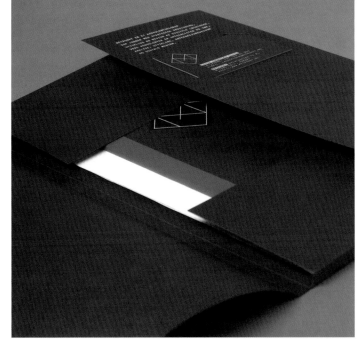

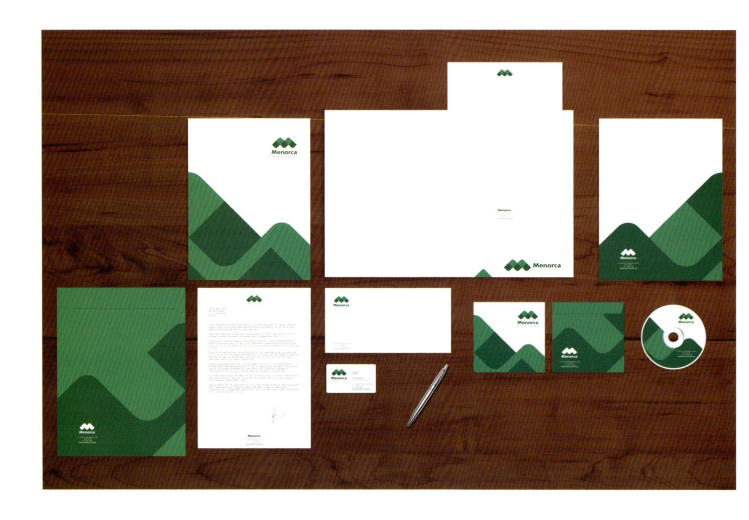

Menorca

Year of Completion_ 2011
Design Firm_ Smart! Grupo Creativo
Photography_ Ignacio Casareto
Client_ Menorca Inversiones

Menorca is a company dedicated to the urban landscapes in Peru. Its growth and scale of completed projects showed the need to create an institutional system that gives identity and coherence to the communication of the company. To this end, a work plan was created to reach not only the development of the visual identity of the brand, but also a strategic integrated communication plan. It included a standardized system of advertising and promotional text and the implementation of signage and graphics in branch offices.

C80 M0 Y100 K20

C100 M0 Y100 K50

Dear Me Brasserie

Year of Completion_ 2012
Designer_ Daniel Ting Chong
Photography_ Daniel Ting Chong
Client_ Dear Me

Dear Me Brasserie is the latest project by South African designer Daniel Ting Chong. It is an all-day brasserie and deli in Cape Town, South Africa. The designer was asked to develop a brand identity and various design collateral. He came up with the name "Dear Me" to give a sense of self-reward when visiting the brasserie.

C80 M36 Y93 K28

C86 M28 Y81 K14

Tim Muldowney Painting

Year of Completion_ 2011
Design Firm_ Jack Muldowney Design Co.
Photography_ Nicole Ziegler
Client_ Tim Muldowney Painting

For an on-the-go client such as Tim, this branding exercise needed to be downright simple. A logo mockup that incorporated all necessary contact info was made into a self-inking stamp. The simplicity of the identity has proven most practical, easily applied to business cards, invoices, note cards, paint chips and more.

AM1000 Studio

Year of Completion_ 2012
Design Firm_ Isabela Rodrigues Sweety Branding Studio
Photography_ Isabela Rodrigues Sweety Branding Studio
Client_ AM1000 Studio

Isabela Rodrigues Sweety Branding Studio always loves pattern and beautiful colors! The AM1000 Studio called the design team for a rebranding, and the designers did this work, as always, with passion. They made some funny patterns that can be printed on several products of stationery and wallpaper.

Petrol Handmade Accessories

Year of Completion_ 2013
Design Firm_ Corn Studio
Photography_ Corn Studio
Client_ Petrol Handmade Accessories

This is a jewelry branding project. The corporate image had to be fresh and innovative without losing the essence of its classic style. The designers accomplished this with calligraphic script lettering combined with the butterfly logo, which refers to freedom and pureness. In this way, they developed a clean and minimal corporate identity in order to reflect modern aesthetics. Cyan and black were chosen as the corporate colors of the brand and implemented in all applications of the identity.

C76 M10 Y60 K0

Montreux Cafe

Year of Completion_ 2010
Design Firm_ BÜRO UFHO
Photography_ Kevin Lim
Client_ Montreux Cafe

BÜRO UFHO rebranded Montreux Cafe to increase its brand awareness. A typeface similar to the previous one is used to help bridge the transition of the rebranding. The element of the wheat symbol was also kept, and used to subtly frame the typography. By varying the thickness of the condensed typeface, the designers are able to compact the word mark as much as possible, yet maximizing legibility.

Mr. & Mrs. Mehlhoff's Wedding Invitation

Year of Completion_ 2011
Designer_ April Larivee
Photography_ April Larivee
Client_ Hillary Mehlhoff

This project is a wedding invitation for a young couple. Uncoated stock embellished with clear pearl foil patterns, silver foil monograms, a wax seal, and a ribbon make this piece appealing to the senses. The beautiful color used in the design gives people a feeling of freshness.

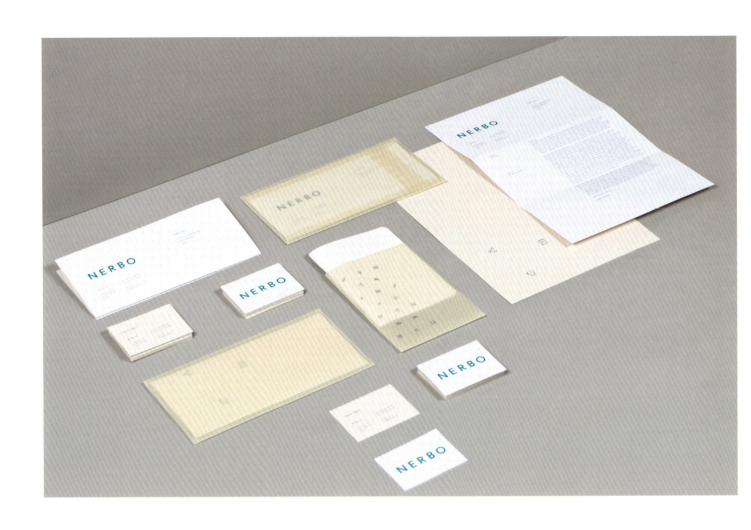

Nerbo

Year of Completion_ 2012
Design Firm_ Augusto Arduini, Giuditta Brusadelli
Photography_ Augusto Arduini, Giuditta Brusadelli
Client_ Nottingham Trent University

The Nerbo project represents the graphic work of Nottingham Trent University's Master Project. The challenge was to create a coffeehouse chain for students from different universities and in different cities. The intriguing and appealing color palette is the pairing of a primary bright aqua with a secondary family of cream colors. The contrast between the warm creaminess of the neutrals and the more "synthetic" force of the aqua is well balanced. To a young person, it is serious but relaxing and engaging at the same time.

COLOUR PALETTE

3E Architecture

Year of Completion_ 2011
Design Firm_ Chad Miller
Photography_ Chad Miller
Client_ 3E Architecture

The project is the brand identity for an architecture firm in Chicago. The three founders of 3E share two things: a surname that begins with the letter "E" and the goal to build great things together. These elements were used as the building blocks for creating the logo.

Hunchworks

Year of Completion_ 2012
Design Firm_ Hyperakt
Client_ Hunchworks

Hunchworks was created at the United Nations' Global Pulse to help find solutions for the world's biggest problems. It is a platform that connects experts around the world, enabling them to collaborate and solve problems on a global scale. As the project continues to develop, Hyperakt is working together with the founders of Hunchworks to give them a brand that meets their goal. All those involved are excited to see the impact of this powerful idea.

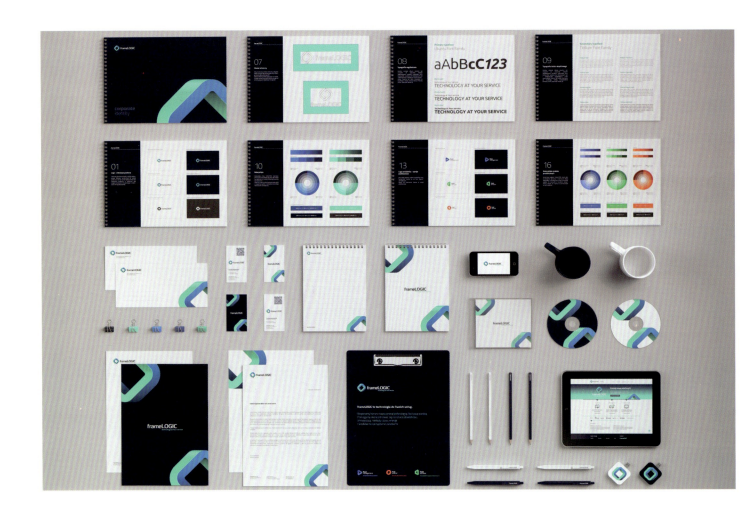

frameLOGIC

Year of Completion_ 2013
Design Firm_ Necon
Photography_ Necon
Client_ frameLOGIC

frameLOGIC is a leading fleet management solutions supplier in Poland. It required a vibrant and professional visual identification system for the whole company. The rebranding project included the creation of not only new corporate materials, but also digital templates of documents, emails, and presentations. A completely new website is one of the biggest elements in the new marketing strategy.

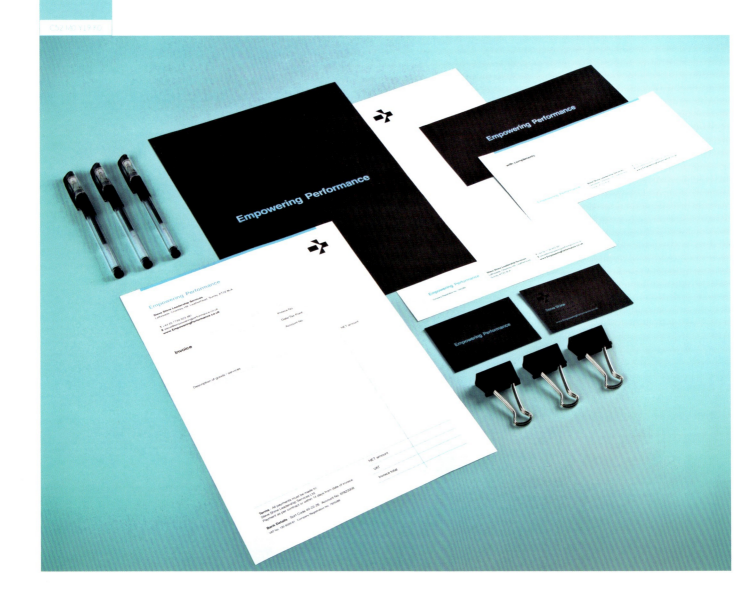

Empowering Performance

Year of Completion_ 2012
Design Firm_ Analogue
Photography_ Mike Johns
Client_ Steve Shine

This project is a personal brand project for Steve Shine. Through several interviews and research, Analogue boiled down Steve's brand essence to "Empowering Performance." This positive and forward-thinking statement was combined with a bold, graphic icon, which encapsulates his progressive and driven nature. The exterior of the business card has an elegant and refined appearance, yet its vivid and electric blue core serves to echo his powerful and positive personality.

Vintage and Cofee for Music

Year of Completion_ 2012
Design Firm_ +Quespacio, Ana Milena Hernández Palacios
Photography_ David Rodríguez Pastor
Client_ Vintage and Cofee for Music

The goal for this project was to create an identity for the interior of Vintage and Cofee for Music that represents the characteristics of the brand through different communication tools. In other words, the goal was to apply the corporate image to the corporate space. The interior space was created to represent the key values of the brand; these values are particularly reflected through the naming and the slogan. Fresh colors applied according to their communicative use present a world full of new sensations and tastes.

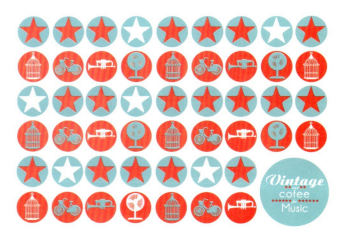

The Greenwich Hotel

Year of Completion_ 2011
Design Firm_ Apartment One
Client_ The Greenwich Hotel

The Greenwich Hotel, Robert DeNiro's 88-room luxury property in TriBeCa NYC, is the premier destination for discerning travelers. Apartment One brought the sophistication of the hotel to its key collateral in print and on the web. They added personal touches to items like the keycard envelope and the Welcome Kit; they refined the logo, corporate stationery, business cards, and other printed materials. Apartment One also revamped the spa menu and collateral for the hotel's notable Shibui Spa.

Officeria

Year of Completion_ 2011
Design Firm_ Kreujemy.to, Piotr Ploch
Photography_ Kreujemy.to
Client_ Sages Sp. z o.o.

Officeria is The Academy of Computer Skills for office workers. The design team wanted to merge school and office into one symbol. They produced a very distinctive symbol, creating a graphic that is an academy heraldry made of a paper clip.

NH Vínculos Comerciales

Year of Completion_ 2012
Design Firm_ +Quespacio, Ana Milena Hernández Palacios
Photography_ David Rodríguez Pastor
Client_ NH Vínculos Comerciales

NH Vínculos Comerciales is an enterprise specialized in representing and introducing European brands to South American markets, with the aim to increase sales from Spanish companies in emerging markets. The lotus symbolizes the rebirth that NH Vínculos Comerciales can offer to Spanish companies, who suffer declining national sales at home, by guiding them in operating in emerging markets. Every petal from the identity is an independent unity that reflects the different areas of the company and their main market specialty.

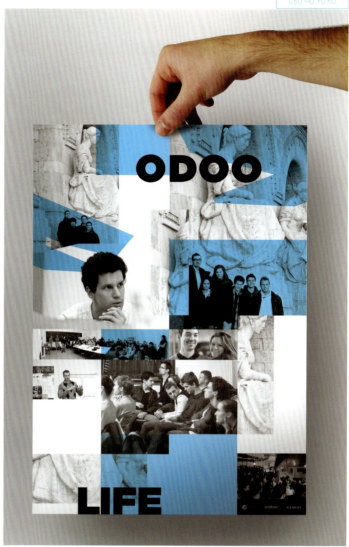

Odooproject

Year of Completion_ 2012
Design Firm_ Hidden Characters, Dániel Nagy, Péter Orbán
Photography_ Dániel Nagy
Client_ Odooproject

The design team created this identity for the Hungarian Solar Decathlon team, who designed and built a house that uses only solar energy. The team's visual communication has a direct connection with the building itself, as well as the sun that operates it. They chose the house and its shadow for an emblem so that, with the phenomenon of the day and night and the seasons' changes, they could create various logo images. This contains endless visual possibilities and characters.

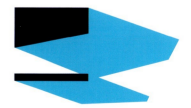

Lisn Music

Year of Completion_ 2011
Design Firm_ Analogue
Photography_ Mike Johns
Client_ Lisn Music

Lisn Music is an online music-licensing library designed for media professionals who need high quality audio to accompany projects they are working on. Analogue was asked to design and create a site that makes both adding and purchasing music as simple as possible in a visually stunning way. To promote the site the agency produced a simple fold-out mailer that housed a CD and reflected their cutting-edge and forwarding-thinking approach to music synchronization.

C100 M0 Y0 K0

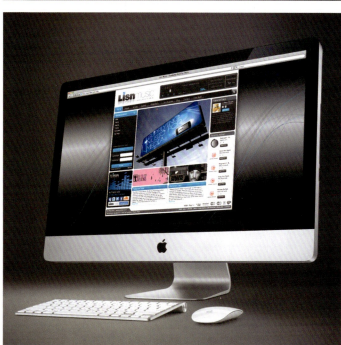

The Peak Lab.

Year of Completion_ 2012
Design Firm_ Katharinamauer.de
Photography_ Maximilian Reinwand
Client_ The Peak Lab.

This is a corporate identity for a technology agency based in Oldenburg, Germany. The dot in the logotype represents an abstract peak generated by the geometric grid, which is part of the identity. The shape is the basic unit of various peaks made of multiple triangles. Each colleague has his own peak on the back side of the identity card. The agency is currently working on an application for smart phones that can read the peaks and then import the contact data automatically into the address-book.

C27 M47 Y0 K0

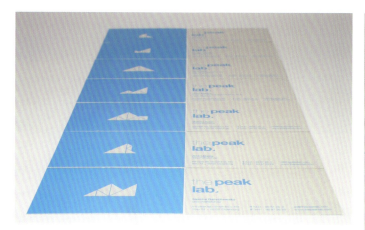

Café du Monde

Year of Completion_ 2011
Design Firm_ lg2boutique
Photography_ Benîot Brühmüllerr
Client_ Café du Monde

lg2boutique refreshed Café du Monde's entire brand identity and created its new communications platform with a focus on the St. Lawrence River, a fun and friendly atmosphere, and the people at the restaurant. This café and its riverside terrace have been a favorite port of call since its opening in 1985. Morning, noon, or night, professionals, artists, lovers, families, and friends gather here to enjoy and enliven the festive atmosphere.

Tobogán

Year of Completion_ 2012
Design Firm_ Marina Senabre Roca,
La Buhardi Architecture & Graphic Design
Photography_ Marina Senabre Roca
Client_ Luis de Coca Serra

The objective of the project was to evidence, in every detail, an environment that combines freshness and elegance, between the calm of Cala Galdana and the quality of a good restaurant. The new brand identity was created based on fluid lines, simple forms, and chromatic simplicity. The combination of fonts (a main one, organic and casual, with a secondary one, simple and sans serif) creates a fresh composition, which is at the same time elegant. The result is a graphic assembly that conveys the dual personality of the space, perfectly defining Tobogán.

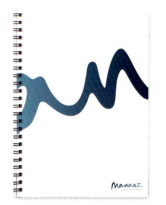

Mannaz

Year of Completion_ 2009
Design Firm_ Scandinavian DesignLab
Photography_ Scandinavian DesignLab
Client_ DIEU

Mannaz is Proto-Germanic and means human. The logo is handwritten, which in itself carries the reference to the focal point of the company — the unique human being. The logo contains both soft and hard values through the combination of the organic form and the cool, blue colors. It is the underlying basis of the entire identity, and an inherent, recurrent visual element in the form of the graphic structure. The style of the photos and the color palette support and express the Scandinavian roots.

Samsung Developers

Year of Completion_ 2012
Design Firm_ Plus X
Photography_ Plus X
Client_ Samsung Electronics

Samsung Developers is a platform brand to share the latest information with developers all over the world. The challenge was to ensure the brand identity and create communication tools such as a new BI to allow interactive communication through its various touch points. The concept of the identity design was "Progressive Platform." It was developed as a flexible identity formed by combination of quadrangles, which symbolizes smart devices, and the use of different patterns, symbolizing various contents.

C100 M80 Y0 K0

C5 M90 Y0 K0

C80 M10 Y0 K0

C0 M75 Y100 K0

Naturally Different

Year of Completion_ 2012
Design Firm_ Farmgroup
Photography_ Farmgroup
Client_ Brewberry Co. Ltd.

Farmgroup conceptualized and designed an entire communication campaign for Hoegaarden's design contest, called "Different by Nature," under the global communication concept of "Naturally Different." The designers wanted to express nature through the look and feel of the materials and printing technique. The color blue gives people a feeling of freshness and also adds vitality.

C100 M72 Y0 K18

C20 M25 Y60 K25

InsureRisk

Year of Completion_ 2011
Design Firm_ Lemongraphic
Photography_ Rayz Ong
Client_ InsureRisk

InsureRisk is a general insurance brokerage firm that provides risk management consulting and insurance solutions to businesses and individuals in Australia. The InsureRisk corporate identity package includes the logo, business card, letterhead, folder, and envelope design.

Vadim Zadorozhny's Vehicle Museum

Year of Completion_ 2011
Design Firm_ Playoff Communication Agency
Photography_ Playoff Communication Agency
Client_ Vadim Zadorozhny's Vehicle Museum

This project is for a vehicle museum in Moscow. To modernize the basic elements of its visual brand, the agency developed a new graphic mark, which is a logical development of the existing one. The continuity of the new brand was a major requirement in the formation of a new visual style. As a part of the project, the agency developed the basic, constant brand elements of business documents, presentation materials, as well as a brand standards manual.

Literary Tea

Year of Completion_ 2012
Designer_ Tiago Campeã
Photography_ Tiago Campeã
Client_ Cerco High School, Ministry of Education and Science

Literary Tea is a poetry event at Cerco High School, with the intention of developing students' skills and providing a venue in which they can participate in literary activities. Based on the metaphors and ornaments of poetry, the whole identity was set in an ornamental typeface, as a system to create metaphors for the logo and the several applications. The global idea was to bring the sensation of a poem: to produce a beautiful and delicate piece, which you can admire, even if you don't fully understand it at first sight.

C100 M85 Y25 K10

C23 M45 Y60 K0

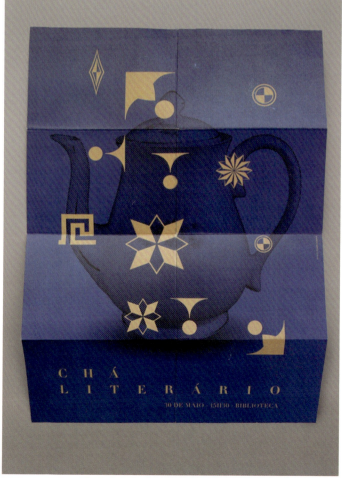

Lucky Brand

Year of Completion_ 2012
Design Firm_ Omnibus Design, Mark Kaiser
Photography_ Omnibus Design
Client_ Lucky Brand

In 2012, Mark Kaiser solidified and refined Lucky Brand's new brand identity and began the application to all print and online materials, including direct mail, advertising, e-commerce, and additional print collateral such as these shown. The program consists of a pocket-sized accordion fold reference guide and a large-format poster of imagery and information. Also shown are two shoe-packaging initiatives. Both are designed to be more eye-catching and brand correct, with subtle but clever copy and a drive to the online presence.

Baltic

Year of Completion_ 2011
Design Firm_ Brunswicker Studio, Mark Brunswicker
Photography_ Frederik Lindstrøm
Client_ Baltic

This work is a full corporate identity including logo, stationery and packaging for the Danish furniture company Baltic. The "behind-the-scenes" mood illustrates the process behind Baltic's production.

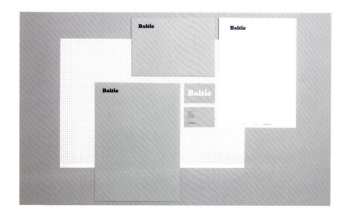

Going Donuts

Year of Completion_ 2012
Design Firm_ Farmgroup
Photography_ Buakaew C. Simmelkjaer
Client_ Going Donuts

This project is for an original American donut shop in Herning, Denmark, which includes branding and an identity package. It's a playful and witty identity system. The designers tried to really express the humor and friendliness of the donut shop through the use of fun sentences and typography.

C100 M80 Y40 K30

C0 M93 Y92 K0

C60 M66 Y57 K46

Lamon Luther

Year of Completion_ 2012
Design Firm_ Russell Shaw Design
Photography_ Micah Lee Bearden, Russell Shaw
Illustration: Jeremy Barnes, Russell Shaw
Client_ Lamon Luther

Lamon Luther, the brand, is a tribute to the memory of the founder's grandfather and all that he stood for — providing for his family by working with his hands. The creations made by the design team utilize reclaimed materials. The company employs formerly homeless craftsmen, giving them an opportunity for new lives. The company workshop exemplifies restoration in every way — preserving the legacy of the rugged gentlemen, and at the same time forging a brand that builds hope for the craftsmen.

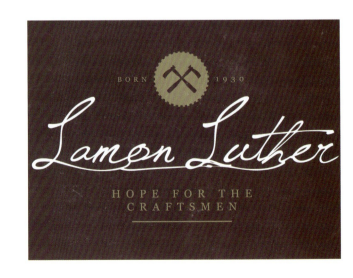

Onkja

Year of Completion_ 2013
Designer_ Piotr Ploch, Motyf
Photography_ Motyf
Client_ Onkja

Onkja is an exclusive Dutch clothing company for kids. The logo designer had to find a way to combine two extreme elements: a child's carefree world and luxury. A rocking horse inscribed inside a crest topped with a crown works perfectly for this brand. The colors used in the design emphasize good feelings related to the brand.

Confeitaria Lopes

Year of Completion_ 2011
Design Firm_ Gen Design Studio
Photography_ Leandro Veloso
Client_ Confeitaria Lopes

Confeitaria Lopes is a traditional bakery and a confectionery at Ponte de Lima city, in northwest Portugal. The intention was to create a homemade identity, with a retro/vintage language, suggesting the chocolate's imagery in the cooking process. The whole project includes visual identity, logo, stationery, and packaging (homemade jam labels, Panettone cake and candy packaging).

C52 M99 Y9 K60

T & Cake

Year of Completion_ 2011
Design Firm_ Build
Photography_ JMWL
Client_ Stephen and Tracy Jackson

Experienced restaurateurs Stephen and Tracy Jackson approached Build to create a brand for their new modern cafe T & Cake based in Yorkshire, UK. They wanted an identity that reflected the quality of the food served, as well as serving to future-proof the identity for use in the retail sector. The seasonality of the cafe's produce is mirrored in the cherry and berry colors in the color palette, and the friendly identity is enhanced by the warm typeface and bite mark.

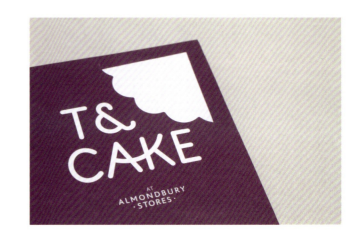

C45 M100 Y0 K55

C0 M100 Y68 K0

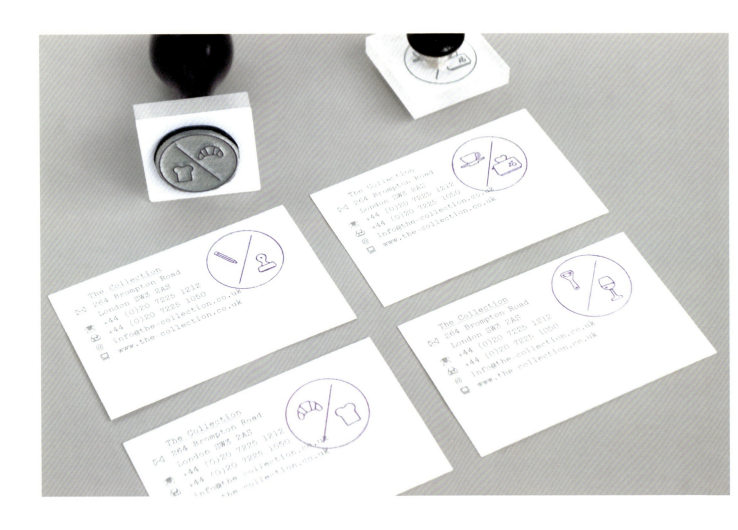

The Collection

Year of Completion_ 2011
Design Firm_ Mind
Client_ The Collection

The Collection is a restaurant, cultural event, and retail space. The idea for the identity relates to multiple prints, limited editions, and artists' signatures. Everything is based on an A5 format with punched holes. Designers used screen printing which allowed them to change colors on the printing bed and make each print unique. Several A5 boards make up larger signs and the thickness is achieved by hanging several signs in front of each other. For the logo, the designers asked the client to write "the collection" in their own handwriting, connecting two dots equivalent to the punched holes.

C92 M95 Y22 K9

C36 M62 Y0 K0

C60 M18 Y0 K0

Megabox

Year of Completion_ 2011
Design Firm_ Studio Fnt
Photography_ Jaemin Lee
Client_ Megabox

This work is the identity design for the Megabox, one of the biggest movie theatre chains in Korea. It includes a symbol, logotype and applications from signage and tickets to beverage. A flexible identity system was created to communicate the movie theatre as an open space for entertainment and communication.

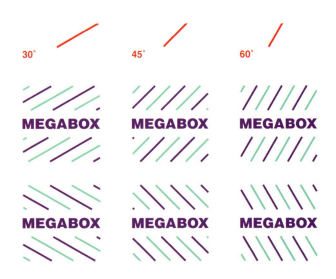

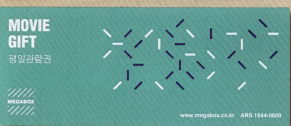
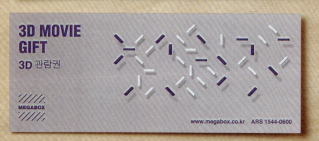

Bespoke Tailoring

Year of Completion_ 2011
Design Firm_ Teacake Design
Photography_ Teacake Design, Sebastian Matthes
Client_ Charles Campbell

Every man needs a tailor, and most tailors need an engaging identity to promote their traditional craft to a modern and sophisticated audience. Teacake Design created the logo using a traditional serif typeface and a traditional line drawing of a master tailor's most important tool — scissors. So far they have produced a set of hand pressed business cards on a stunning lilac color in a robust 540g. Also included in the design package are a full website, product packaging, carrier bags, shirt boxes, and silk tie envelopes.

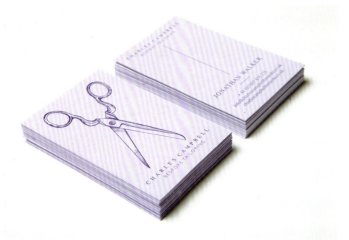

C56 M60 Y2 K0

The Flower Company

Year of Completion_ 2011
Design Firm_ Piotr Ploch
Photography_ Piotr Ploch
Client_ The Flower Company

The Flower Company is a floral design studio creating bouquets for all kinds of celebrations. Designing a stylish logo was the designer's goal. He wanted a floral motive to be included in the logo in a way that would clearly indicate the company's style. The result is a flower made of interlacing ribbons. The floral ribbon was used in many components of the company's visual identification. Flowers also inspired the colors used in this identity.

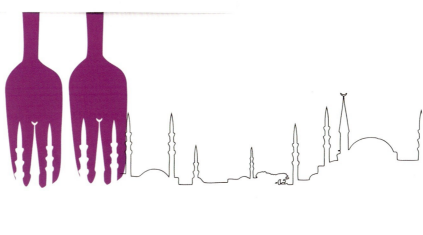

Doner Kebab

Year of Completion_ 2011
Design Firm_ +Quespacio, Ana Milena Hernández Palacios
Photography_ Cualiti
Client_ Doner Kebab

Fast food snack bar Doner Kebab needed to modernize its image to attract the young Ibiza tourist market. The brand is represented by a corporate identity that integrates key aspects from Doner Kebab's business, an Arabian city, and the rotating grilled meat. Through bold color the design is successful at attracting their young, modern audience, who are between 20 and 35 years old.

Sandra's Haarschnitt

Year of Completion_ 2012
Design Firm_ Katharinamauer.de
Photography_ Kilian Kessler
Client_ Thomas Speiser Gestaltung

This is a corporate identity for "Sandra's Haarschnitt" — a stylist based in Zürich, Switzerland. The idea behind the logo was to create a pair of scissors out of the letter "S" in the name "Sandra." The color and the typeface stand for a modern, feminine style that characterizes the attitude of the hairstylist.

Art Fabrica

Year of Completion_ 2010
Design Firm_ Playoff Communication Agency
Photography_ Playoff Communication Agency
Client_ Art Fabrica

The main focus of the company Art Fabrica is architecture and engineering. In its old visual corporate identity, each of the units was a distinctive element in the overall style. The new visual style of the brand Art Fabrica reflects two main ideas: First, the company is working with space and form; secondly, the company provides a wide range of services.

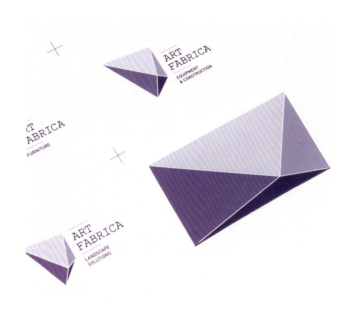

Monkey with Guns

Year of Completion_ 2012
Design Firm_ ICK Studio
Photography_ Mauricio Bigliante
Client_ Monkey with Guns Film Company

Monkey with Guns is an independent film company based in Las Vegas, USA. The company was born from the need to showcase the brand's true nature though impeccable stories. It is a film factory fueled by throughts, ideas and concepts, and undertakes attractive projects that flirt at both art and business. ICK Studio was challenged with designing a strong visual and conceptual identity that represents independence, resourcefulness, and effectiveness in getting the job done. Colors and typography combine seamlessly in a neat fashion to illustrate a dynamic and highly professional business attitude.

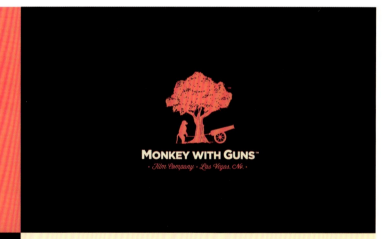

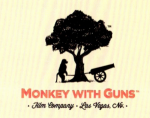

Artspace

Year of Completion_ 2011
Design Firm_ Apartment One
Client_ Ben Alsop

Artspace is an online contemporary-art marketplace that easily allows art lovers to become art collectors. Apartment One developed the core brand identity, e-commerce website, print and marketing collateral, and consumer packaging. They sought to create a visual language that conveys sophistication and refinement while remaining accessible, and a framework within which to showcase art. The result: a largely black palette infused with neon pink that brings vibrancy and modernism to the brand.

C0 M90 Y0 K0

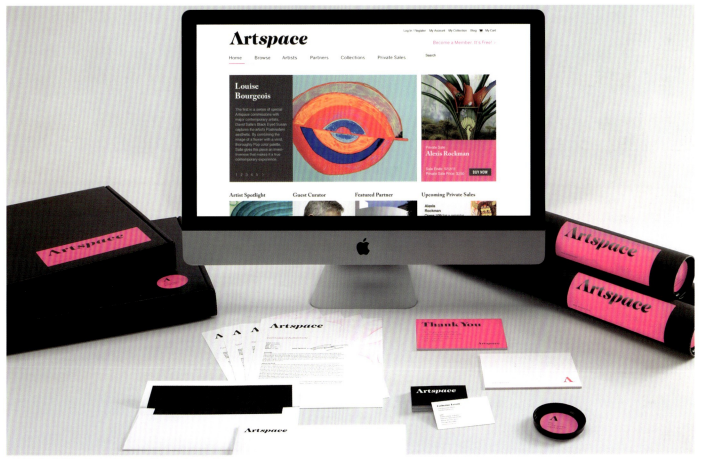

Flor Aguilar's Personal Identity

Year of Completion_ 2013
Designer_ Flor Aguilar
Photography_ Flor Aguilar
Client_ Flor Aguilar

To create her own personal identity, the designer aspired to reflect the two favorite things she focuses on: identity and illustration. She created a simple but smart logo with the two first letters of her name, which was the basis for the logotype and included an illustration that reflects her ideas and feelings about design. She really thinks this represents her as a designer and even as an individual, which gives this project a genuine "identity."

C=0
M=90
Y=10
K=0

R=238
G=61
B=138

PANTONE 806 U

Black

C10 M100 Y17 K20

Econcern

Year of Completion_ 2008
Design Firm_ Scandinavian DesignLab
Client_ Econcern

The task was to create and set a new standard for a new visual identity, which was as unique, unconventional, and unrivalled as the company itself, and at the same time create space for future accomplishments. The logo consists of two elements: a monogram and an abstract symbol in a very unconventional choice of color. The symbol, which is made up of the existing letters in the monogram composed in a new way, thus represents Econcern's solutions.

Jazzy Innovations

Year of Completion_ 2012
Design Firm_ Alicja Wydmanska
Photography_ Alicja Wydmanska
Client_ Jazzy Innovations

Jazzy Innovations is an IT development company from Poland. At first they only wanted a new web design, but while checking their identity the designers decided to create something new and more professional for the company. The designers have created for them a completely new corporate identity package, including a web site, mobile version of the site, office interiors, and advertising materials.

Sladunitsa

Year of Completion_ 2012
Designer_ Alex Matveev
Photography_ Alex Matveev
Client_ Sladunitsa Confectionery Factory

Sladunitsa is one of the largest confectionery manufacturers in Siberia. The designer focused on considering all touch points between the company and customers. This culminated in a project where he created the complete visual identity, including logotype and corporate communications, as well as packaging and office navigation elements. By using a beautiful illustrative style complemented with a modern yet warm typeface, he was able to be consistent with the brand look and feel, allowing the brand to be communicated to the staff and consumers with feelings of belonging and loyalty.

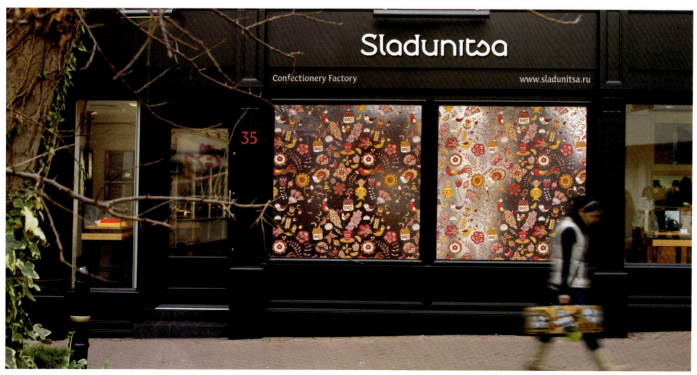

International Game Days

Year of Completion_ 2012
Designer_ Stefan Zimmermann
Photography_ Stefan Zimmermann
Client_ Bachelor Thesis at the FH Aachen, University of Applied Sciences

Stefan Zimmermann developed a corporate design concept for the International Game Days in Essen, Germany. This annual fair is the world's largest trade event for board games. The target of the thesis was to design an identity concept with a distinctive hallmark, a uniform layout, and to create a concept for marketing campaigns. The appearance should fit to the topic of play and to the high standard of the fair. Abstraction, interaction, and variability are central ideas of each game. The corporate design reflects those aspects and strengthens the new visual identity.

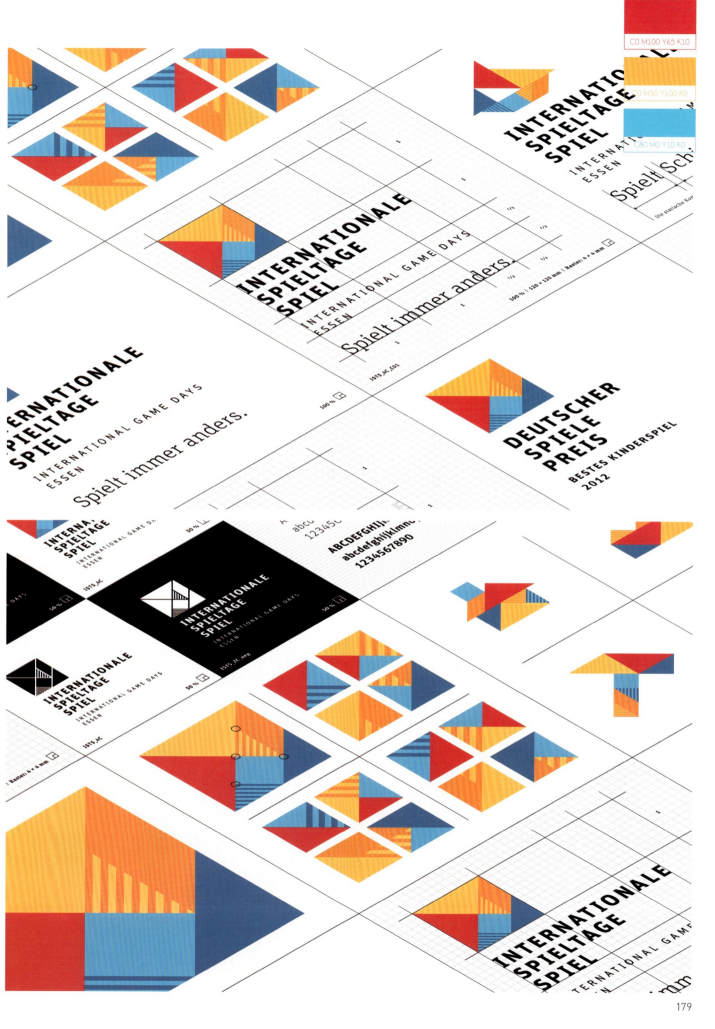

Anoniwa Corporate Stationary

Year of Completion_ 2012
Design Firm_ Anoniwa, Naoto Kitaguchi
Photography_ Yuka Yamaguchi
Client_ Original Work

These are designs for Anoniwa. The emblem, consisting of two trees, and the sun and moon on the company's site, are created as a symbol of the brand to evoke emotions of eternal joint cooperation with clients. The identity was also designed in a whimsical way, intended to be seen as many different things, such as a winking or surprised face, to convey that Anoniwa is also a place that can have fun with many different ideas.

www.anoniwa.jp

Soul Kitchen

Year of Completion_ 2011
Design Firm_ Apartment One
Client_ Soul Kitchen

Soul Kitchen is a "community restaurant" in Red Bank, New Jersey, founded by Dorothea and Jon Bon Jovi. Apartment One developed a vibrant, expressive brand-identity system that encapsulates the founders' vision and appeals to a diverse audience. They created an inspirational motto, Hope Is Delicious, and a brand manifesto that speaks to the ideals of the Kitchen. Apartment One designed print and marketing collateral, as well as the website utilizing handcrafted type, bright brand colors, and a "human, soulful" approach.

Piccino

Year of Completion_ 2012
Design Firm_ +Quespacio, Ana Milena Hernández Palacios
Photography_ David Rodríguez Pastor
Client_ Piccino

The challenge for this project was to design the corporate identity for a kids' store, starring two young kids that are continually inviting new friends to visit their store. In addition to the design of a logotype, two children's characters were created to be part of the marketing communication of the shop. The two kids take an active communication role, aiming to attract new little clients through a joyful, juvenile image with colors that never cease to claim the attention of any child.

Yoshida Design

Year of Completion_ 2012
Design Firm_ Lundgren+Lindqvist
Photography_ Kalle Sanner
Client_ Yoshida Design

Yoshida Design is an architectural practice based in Oslo, Norway, whose founder is originally from Osaka, Japan. The business cards are printed in four different colors and edge-printed, following the color coding of the different document types, on sturdy Munken Lynx paper. With two different grided backs for personal notes, the cards also allow for use as correspondence cards.

Dilly Dally

Year of Completion_ 2011
Design Firm_ Spring
Photography_ Spring
Client_ Dilly Dally Toy Store

A children's store "inspires play." So much so that every one of the brand's touch points is an extension of this motto. It's been mentioned in numerous design publications, picked up a Lotus Award, Communication Arts Award and was a finalist at The One Show. The use of different colors makes the entire design lively, much like what childhood is meant to be.

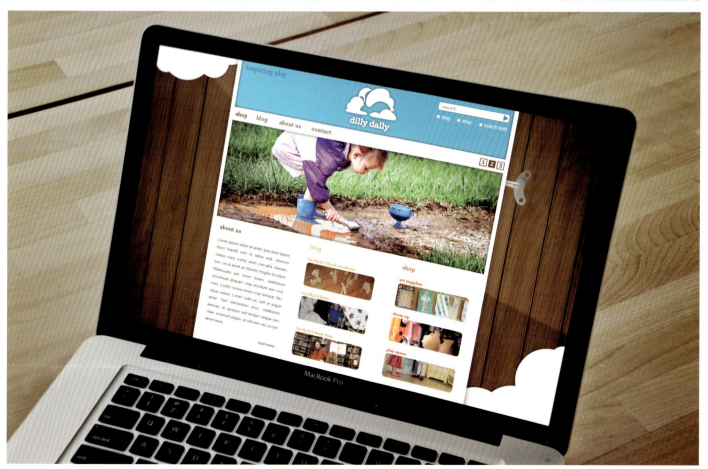

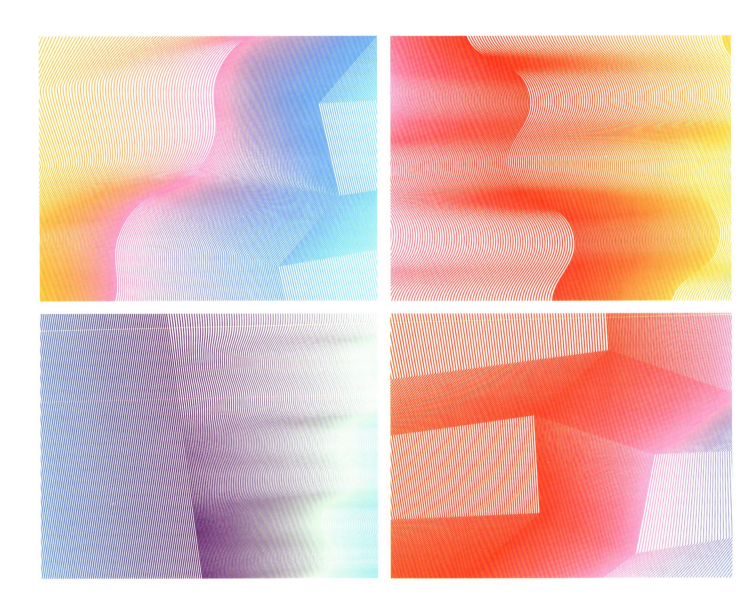

Rítmia Music Therapy

Year of Completion_ 2012
Design Firm_ Atipus
Photography_ Atipus
Client_ Celia Castillo

This project is an identity for social music therapist and educator Celia Castillo. The identity is based on rhythmic exercises that Celia develops. The aim is to create different moods in her patients. A variety of colors were applied in the design so that the identity gives people a feeling of change, which is like a wave reflecting their moods.

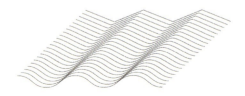

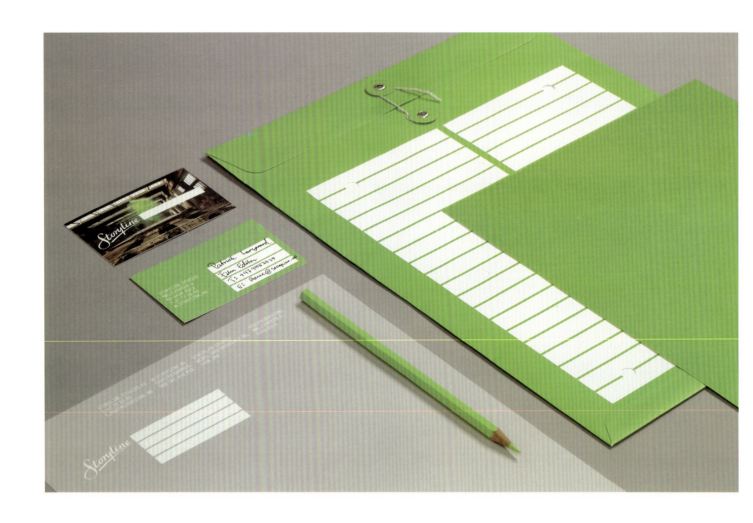

Storyline

Year of Completion_ 2012
Design Firm_ Work in Progress, Torgeir Hjetland
Photography_ Filippo Minelli
Client_ Storyline Studios

The project includes identity, interior design, a signage system and art direction for Norway's largest film studio. The name also implies a full-scale film production — people's notion of film and commercials is an escape, a twist on reality, exciting action, and colorful special effects. The photos taken for the identity are frozen moments where the future is yet to be revealed, and it makes the viewer engaged and curious.

C0 M85 Y0 K0

C0 M15 Y100 K0

C85 M25 Y0 K0

C60 M0 Y100 K0

Vrrb Interactive

Year of Completion_ 2011
Design Firm_ FRVR
Photography_ FRVR
Client_ Vrrb Interactive

Vrrb Interactive is a California-based, web-developing start-up. FRVR came up with an identity concept based on a strong, custom-made logotype. The logotype is used together with a color system based on an existing set of colored papers. Using pre-made colored papers allowed the designers to use a wide range of colors in print applications without raising the print price or lowering the color quality by printing them in non-spot colors.

Brighton Road Studios

Year of Completion_ 2012
Design Firm_ Glad Creative
Photography_ Ant Tran
Client_ Brighton Road Studios

Brighton Road Studios is a grade II listed building that provides collaborative workspaces for creative practitioners in Gateshead, England. Designers created a brand, fully content-managed website, signage and invitations. The logo features a "B" which is formed out of various combinations of shapes and colors, representing the creative possibilities that can result from the occupants sharing space, ideas and working collaboratively. Although the logo appears in hundreds of combinations, the core look and feel of the branding remains distinctive.

Waldo Trommler Paints

Year of Completion_ 2012
Design Firm_ Reynolds and Reyner
Photography_ Artyom Kulik, Alexander Andreyev
Client_ Waldo Trommler Paints

"We don't just need, we must stand out." This phrase has become the basis at work on a new brand identity — Waldo Trommler Paints. WTP is not just a manufacturer of paints, it's an assistant, always ready to help, suggest, and defend its clients from hassles and problems. It has no corporate colors, but the corporate identity is common for each design element, from business cards to packaging. Every item is a bright and memorable combination of colors and objects that all together form a whole — the entire brand.

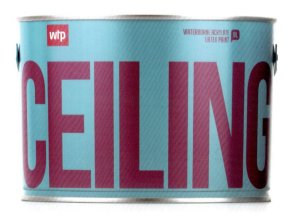

Le Bilboquet Laurier

Year of Completion_ 2011
Design Firm_ Sébastien Bisson
Photography_ Sébastien Bisson
Client_ Le Bilboquet Laurier

Le Bilboquet is a Montreal-based artistic ice cream maker. Since its creation in 1983, the key corporate objective has been to produce the highest quality of ice creams and sorbets possible in a fun and enjoyable environment. Their priority has always been to develop an environmentally friendly product with reutilization and recycling. The brand identity reflects the idea of fun and freshness with a human touch.

Bumsies

Year of Completion_ 2012
Design Firm_ Berger & Föhr
Photography_ Jamie Kripke
Client_ Bumsies

Bumsies is an organic baby clothing line inspired by the heart of Bali. Through the simple act of purchasing a Bumsies product you can create real, positive change in the world. Bumsies sales are donated to Bumi Sehat, a non-profit, village-based health organization in Bali and Aceh, Indonesia.

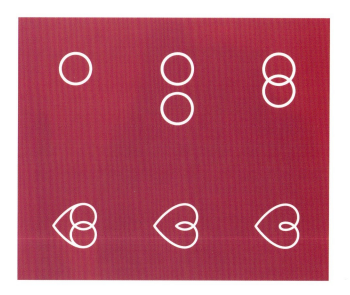

Marawa — The Amazing

Year of Completion_ 2010
Design Firm_ Mind Design
Client_ Marawa — The Amazing

This is the identity for Marawa — The Amazing, an internationally well-known Hula Hoop artist and performer. The logo is based on the Revue theatre display fonts, which often use light bulbs. The stationery is printed in many variations using three Pantone colors as well as black and white images, and every business card is different.

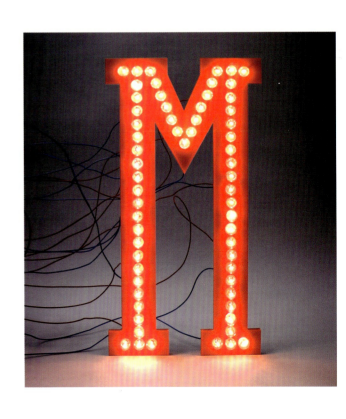

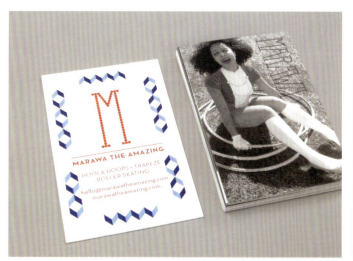

Chocolat Factory

Year of Completion_ 2003-2012
Design Firm_ Ruiz+Company
Client_ Chocolat Factory

Chocolat Factory is a top quality chocolate brand with 40 shops of its own throughout Spain. Ruiz+Company handled the brand's corporate identity and the design of its packaging, creating a powerful and original graphic code that moved away from the classic image types for these sorts of products. The result was a unique brand identity with loads of personality.

C30 M96 Y72 K30

C0 M70 Y85 K0

C65 M40 Y90 K30

Victoria Harley

Year of Completion_ 2012
Design Firm_ Fettle
Photography_ Victoria Harley
Client_ Victoria Harley

This is the brand and identity work for the brilliant UK photographer, Victoria Harley. The identity system includes a custom-drawn monogram that can be applied to stationery using a range of printing techniques and processes. Business cards were letter-pressed at E.E Chrisp on 500gsm beer-mat board. Letterheads were litho printed at E.E Chrisp on Gmund 135gsm Bier Weizen. Two ink stamps and a hand embosser were created to customize stationery and authenticate prints. Envelopes are GF Smith Dark Grey Colorplan.

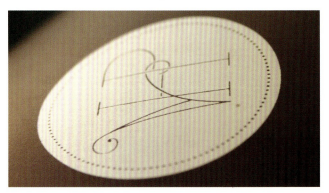

Camping de Dalt

Year of Completion_ 2012
Design Firm_ Marina Senabre Roca, La Buhardi Architecture & Graphic Design
Photography_ Marina Senabre Roca
Client_ Grup Municipal Compromís

"Camping de Dalt" is a proposal for a local urban campsite. The campsite is a place of relationships among its users, and also between those users and the environment. It has a beautiful feature: the absence of limits. The limit is only a fictitious line established for technical purposes. But if left to expand, the campsite could do so infinitely. The urban campsite is notable for its interesting duality: nature and city; introverted, but connected; a place to relax, but next to the city. It was important that the brand identity of the campsite was able to convey this duality.

Frederik Lindstrøm

Year of Completion_ 2012
Design Firm_ Brunswicker Studio, Mark Brunswicker
Photography_ Frederik Lindstrøm
Client_ Frederik Lindstrøm

In modernizing photographer Frederik Lindstrøm's visual identity, the studio kept his minimal aesthetic and fondness for Helvetica at the heart of a design solution that encompasses logo, stationery, a portfolio and website.

Glad Creative

Year of Completion_ 2011
Design Firm_ Glad Creative
Photography_ Ant Tran
Client_ Glad Creative

Designers think it's important that as a branding and design agency, their own brand is engaging and memorable. Otherwise, how can they expect clients to believe that they can do so for them? The Glad brand provides an opportunity to have a bit of fun with language, adding wit and personality to each communication.

Lakomi

Year of Completion_ 2011
Design Firm_ Atipo
Photography_ Atipo
Client_ Lakomi

Lakomi is an online shop selling quality prepared food, pasteurized, and processed without preservatives. The naming came from the abbreviation of the term "la comida" (food in Spanish), which combined Spanish origin with the Oriental sound "k." The product is the protagonist in the design, thanks to a sober, white packaging where messages, with some winks of humor, are complicit with the customer.

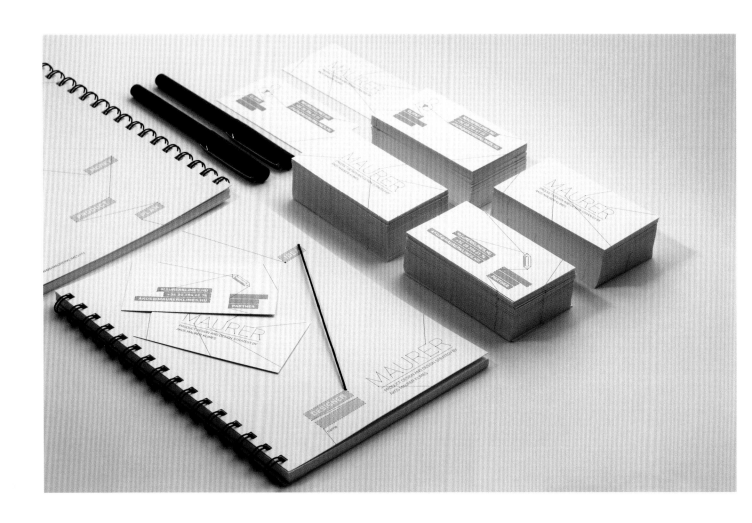

Maurer

Year of Completion_ 2011
Design Firm_ Hidden Characters, Dániel Nagy, Péter Orbán
Photography_ Dániel Nagy
Client_ Ákos Maurer Klimes

The base of the design made for Ákos Maurer Klimes products was to demonstrate the strategic way of thinking. The design team presented how they can get from point A to point B if Ákos draws the line between the two points. Ákos' sketchbook and his favorite design philosophical movement, the Super Normal, defined the visual appearance. The designers dissolved the strict and unified designed system with personal gestures and games in order to make it more direct and friendly.

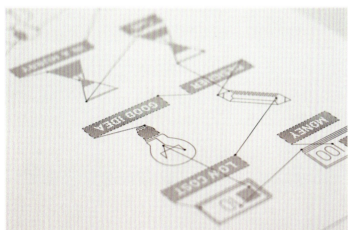

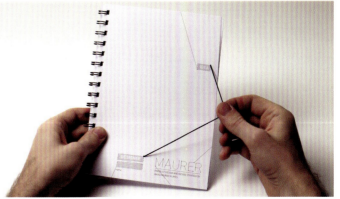

TIN CAN

Year of Completion_ 2012
Design Firm_ COOEE
Photography_ COOEE
Client_ TIN CAN

TIN CAN is a Dutch production company that focuses on the development and production of formats in the field of television, branding, online visuals, and events. The entire identity consists of two basic elements that constitute the logo — a basic typography with four basic lines. Each line refers to one of the four disciplines of their profession. These lines are the main "format" for the entire identity and are adaptable to different types of content and applications.

C0 M8 Y9 K80

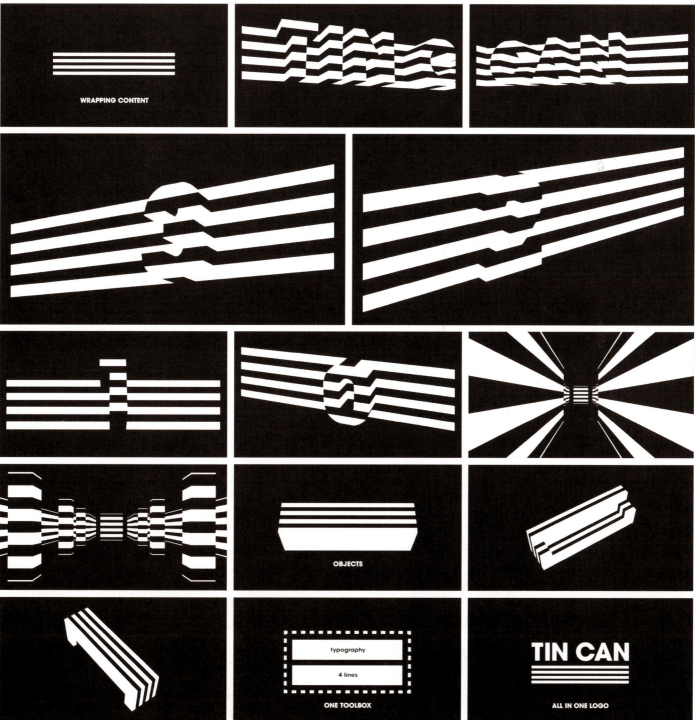

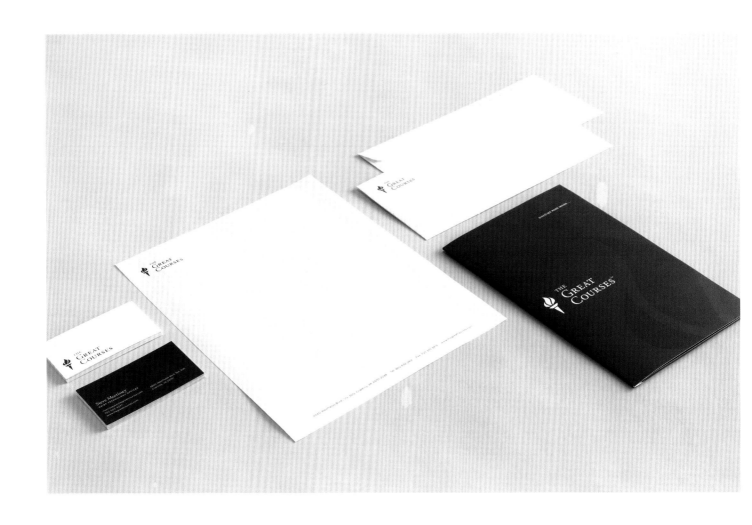

The Great Courses

Year of Completion_ 2011
Design Firm_ Apartment One
Client_ The Great Courses

For over 20 years, the Great Courses has been a trusted source for multimedia educational courses led by the world's best professors. Apartment One revitalized the brand, expanding its appeal to a wider audience while maintaining the trust of its core consumers. They completed a full-scale digital and print redesign that included packaging, catalogs, advertisements, and marketing e-mails. The designers created a new logo and visual identity, and developed a color-coded packaging system for all of their courses.

C72 M60 Y50 K35

C58 M40 Y100 K20

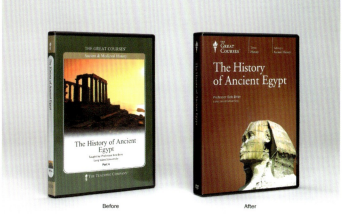

Before   After

211

John Casablanca's International Institute

Year of Completion_ 2012
Design Firm_ Spring
Photography_ Spring
Client_ John Casablanca's International Institute

Widely recognized as an industry leader, John Casablanca's International Institute has set the standard for artistry and innovation since 1978. Working with the literal translation of "casablanca," meaning "white house," the institute's logo depicts the architecture of a house, conveying a sense of belonging and security. Disciplines are differentiated from one another with unique graphic treatments. The shapes of the logos are bold and modern: a visual representation of the innovation and creativity that defines JCI Institute.

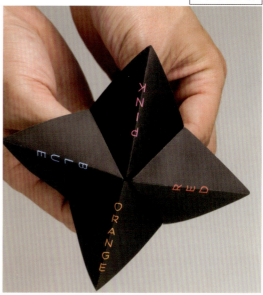

MEDNUT — Tigernut Orxata

Year of Completion_ 2012
Design Firm_ Cinking Studio
Photography_ Cinking Studio
Client_ Proposal for a New Brand

"Orxata" is an artisanal drink typical of Spain. The project's goal was to give it the value it really deserves as a star product of the Mediterranean culture. The designers intended to revamp this product through a high-quality, luxurious and prestigious international brand. MEDNUT is the new orxata chain that they propose, dedicated to the production, sale, and promotion of traditional orxata.

C0 M0 Y0 K100

C0 M0 Y0 K0

Noeeko ID

Year of Completion_ 2011
Design Firm_ Noeeko
Photography_ Michal Sycz
Client_ Noeeko ID

Noeeko's old identity and stationery were designed a few years ago. The main aim of this project was to create a strong and clean brand while keeping the whole design simple, fresh, and interesting. The designers developed an additional pixel art animation, used on the website, to give it a more playful touch and friendly feeling.

C60 M40 Y40 K100

C25 M18 Y68 K0

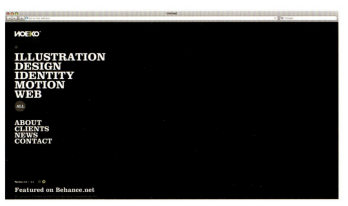

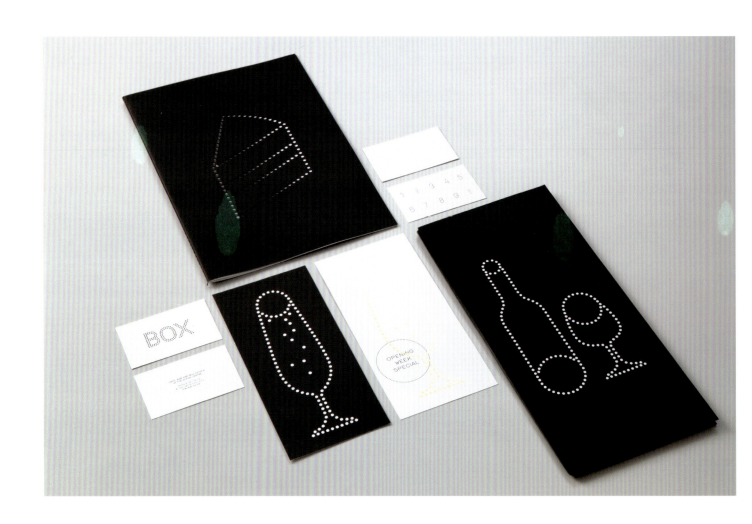

Box Cafe

Year of Completion_ 2011
Design Firm_ Alt Group
Photography_ Toaki Okano
Client_ The Edge

Box Cafe is a key element of the Aotea Square refurbishment project. It is located at the entry of Aotea Centre and functions as an information center, ticketing office and venue. Both the name and visual identity need to simply communicate the offering. The mark lends itself to a range of executions and finishes; it can be printed, embossed, recessed or floated. The identity is implemented throughout signage, uniforms, collaterals, and advertising campaigns.

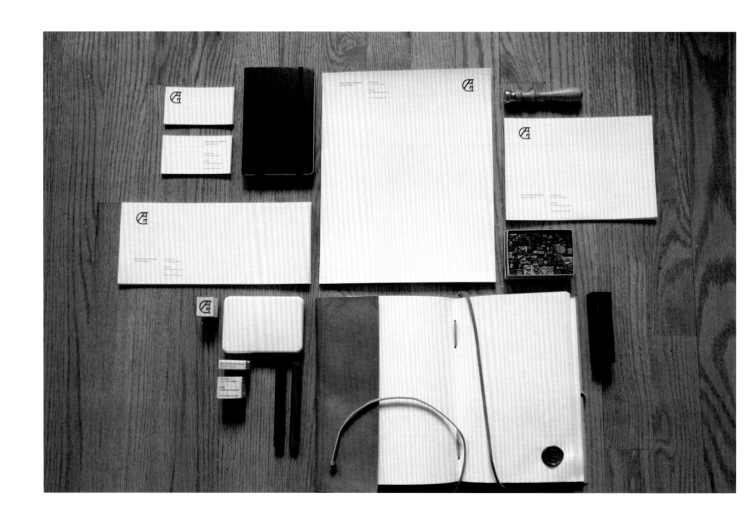

AG

Year of Completion_ 2011
Designer_ Ana Gomez Bernaus
Photography_ Ana Gomez Bernaus
Client_ Ana Gomez Bernaus

As a Barcelona born and raised graphic designer living in New York City, Ana's work breathes both cultures. The Catalan Modernism taught her about composition, attention to details and ornamentation. The practicality that rules the Big Apple brought a more logical and rational approach to her work. This project is a corporate identity for the designer herself. The color scheme of black and white makes it brief and charming.

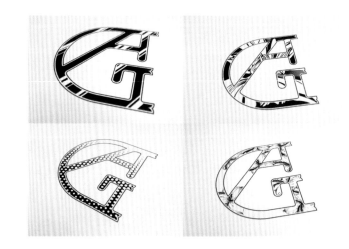

C0 M0 Y0 K100

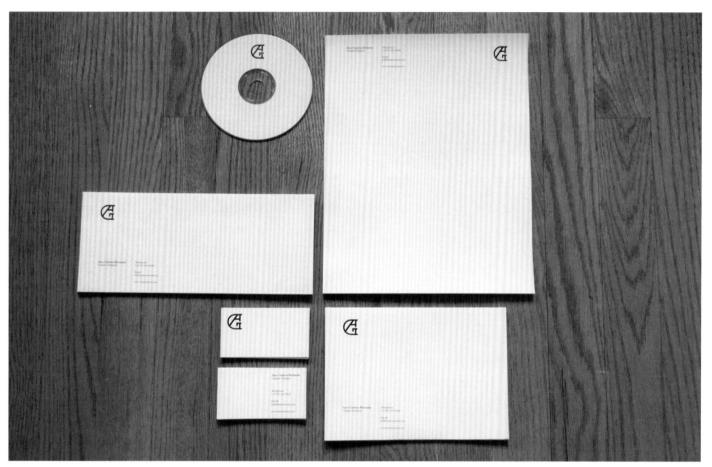

Ravens Heaven

Year of Completion_ 2011
Design Firm_ Farmgroup
Photography_ Farmgroup
Client_ Universal Wings Limited Partnership

This is an identity design for a boutique fashion designer in Thailand. Ravens Heaven's concept revolves around Christianity, Gothic art, and religious belief. The elongated custom logotype suggests the idea of "reaching for heaven" as in the Gothic architecture. The print materials attempt to express the mysterious contrast between ravens and heaven.

Hyde Park Brewery

Year of Completion_ 2011
Designer_ Pawel Adamek
Photography_ Pawel Adamek
Client_ Personal Work

This project was to produce the branding, identity, and packaging for a small ale brewery called "Hyde Park Brewery" in the UK. The aim of the project was to widen the audience of ale drinkers and make ale appeal to younger people. The approach was to use a universal theme across the range of ales that relates to everyone — the seasons. A combination of typography and appropriate seasonal color palette helps form the identity of the brand.

Lise Madore

Year of Completion_ 2010
Design Firm_ lg2boutique
Client_ Lise Madore

The branding is based on a creative strategy to unite the Lise Madore agency's photographers and illustrators within the framework of a change of governance. The art direction is clearly timeless elegance, and serves as a testament to the power of the network.

Hörst

Year of Completion_ 2011
Design Firm_ lg2boutique
Photography_ Marie-Reine Mattera
Client_ Ango Mode

The Hörst branding positions the high-end men's clothing as an authentic brand that brings together romanticism and elegance. Inspired by the modern dandy, the photos feature men who have an elegance and mystery about them and a penchant for excess and extravagance — like any dandy would. All graphic elements were created to highlight both the brand's rich German heritage and its modern style.

MORE Bike Park

Year of Completion_ 2012
Design Firm_ FEB Design + FIBA Design
Photography_ FEB Design + FIBA Design
Client_ Esquio Mountain Reserve

Having high-speed downhill bicycle sports as the main theme, the designers suggested an identity born from the direct synergy between illustration and typography (The black-letter logotype is a custom-made type). The use of illustrations enhanced the story-telling capability of the brand, enabling the designers to explore primary instinct images as stimulant entertainment in order to establish an emotional bridge with the end users.

C0 M0 Y0 K100

C0 M30 Y100 K0

Rock the Vote

Year of Completion_ 2012
Design Firm_ Apartment One
Photography_ Cobra Snake
Client_ Rock the Vote

Apartment One teamed up with Rock the Vote and Simon Isaacs to develop the brand and creative for the "We Will" campaign, one of the largest non-partisan youth voter campaigns in history. The campaign empowered the youth to make their voice heard in the coming election. It was inspired by trends in youth activism and branding to build a campaign that reflected the vision behind "We Will," stayed true to Rock the Vote's mission, and could be shared virtually.

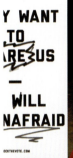

The Danish String Quartet

Year of Completion_ 2012
Designer_ Maibritt Lind Hansen
Photography_ Caroline Bittencourt
Client_ The Danish String Quartet

The Danish String Quartet identity was inspired by the classical era mixed with aesthetics of modern design to create something simple, yet sophisticated. A quartet equals four people, aka the number four. Several elements from the visual language of the written classical music were adopted into the number creating a unique four. You can see the bow, the head of a string instrument, the strings, fingerboard, and the sheets used for writing scores in the symbol.

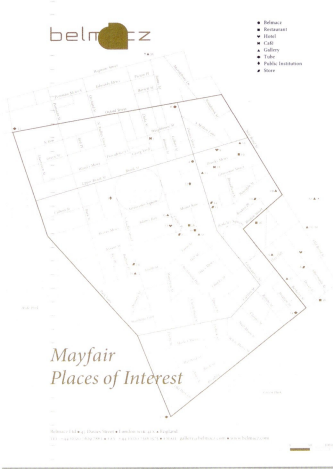

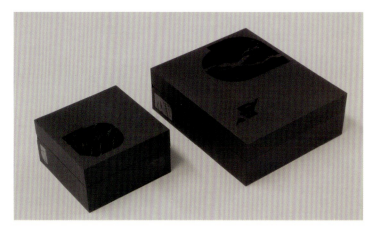

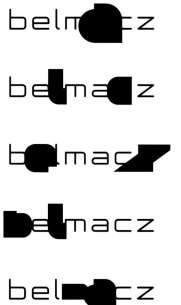

Belmacz

Year of Completion_ 2011
Design Firm_ Mind Design
Client_ Belmacz

Belmacz is a London-based jewelry company that opened its first shop and gallery in the Mayfair area of London. The identity takes Mind Design's original logo but makes it thicker, with "raw" letter shapes. The new Belmacz identity is a complex system of connections and works across different items and media. Every shape that has been cut out on one item of communication reappears on another. For example, a shape missing on a business card can reappear on a carrier bag.

Black Cow Vodka

Year of Completion_ 2012
Design Firm_ Mind Design
Client_ Black Cow Vodka

Mind Design designed the overall identity and bottle for Black Cow Vodka, which is made from milk in the Dorset countryside. The logo was inspired by branding irons used for cattle. It is this brief and cute image that arouses people's curiosity and makes them want to know more about Black Cow Vodka.

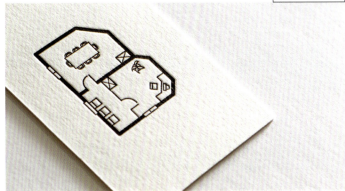

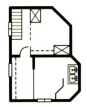

Brass Developments

Year of Completion_ 2011
Design Firm_ Glad Creative
Photography_ Ant Tran
Client_ Brass Developments

Glad Creative created this identity for Brass Developments, a building and property development firm based in northeast England. The new identity, based on building plan illustrations, provides a flexible system which integrates the company's two divisions: Brass Developments Residential and Brass Developments Commercial.

Grebban Design AB

Year of Completion_ 2011
Designer_ Emil Karlsson
Photography_ Emil Karlsson
Client_ Grebban Design AB

Grebban was initially just a web agency based in Skövde, Sweden. In 2011, they took the step to include graphic design to their services and wanted to simultaneously change their graphic identity. The identity was developed into two graphic elements: "Grebban" and the G split in half as a sign of the two units.

Work & Play

Year of Completion_ 2010
Design Firm_ Brunswicker Studio, Mark Brunswicker
Photography_ Frederik Lindstrøm
Client_ Work&Play

Brunswicker Studio created the Danish brand Work & Play's visual identity, including logo and packaging, which meets its goal of targeting young, creative shoppers around the globe.

Bërthama

Year of Completion_ 2011
Design Firm_ projectGRAPHICS
Photography_ projectGRAPHICS
Client_ Bërthama Ltd.

The main idea was to describe the services of the company within the Bërthama logo. Three triangles, drafted as rays, represent different business information sources. The use of black and white characterizes the idea of the work, which symbolically would be that the hidden and unknown are illuminated and become known. The overall image of the logo looks like an eye that sees in three dimensions and what it sees reflects its surrounding space.

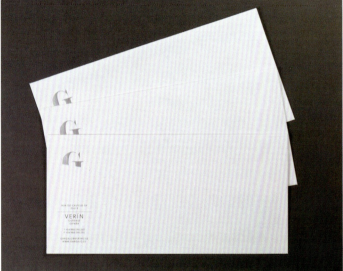

Gargalo

Year of Completion_ 2012
Design Firm_ Solo
Photography_ Solo
Client_ Gargalo

This project includes the redesign and packaging for the company owned by the well-known fashion designer Roberto Verino. The initial concept was born from the special situation of the wine house, residing on a slanted hill, under the impressive castle of Monterrey. Consistent elegance is across the pieces, from the stationary and packaging to the communication items.

Knucklehead Musik

Year of Completion_ 2011
Design Firm_ Kreujemy.to, Piotr Ploch
Photography_ Kreujemy.to
Client_ Knucklehead Musik

Knucklehead Musik is a small music label in Los Angeles uniting hip-hop artists. The rough, street style of the label's productions had to find its way into the project. This is how the design team created a very distinctive symbol illustrating knuckles combined with a vinyl record. The sign was designed in the way which allows it to be used without typography.

Local 360

Year of Completion_ 2011
Design Firm_ Sleep Op
Photography_ Don Milgate
Client_ Marcus Charles

Seattle restaurant Local 360 needed their visual identity built from the ground up, and wanted to blend a turn-of-the-century mercantile vibe with a refined culinary experience. The resulting look is rustic, handcrafted, and elegant. The print approach reinforces the brand principles by using locally hand-printed letterpress business cards and 100% recycled paper for all menus and signage.

Nikolaj Kunsthal

Year of Completion_ 2011
Design Firm_ Scandinavian DesignLab
Client_ Nikolaj Kunsthal

Nikolaj Kunsthal (Nikolaj Contemporary Art Centre) is an art centre in inner Copenhagen, located in a former church from the 12th century. The task was to create an identity, which expresses the mission of the art center, while at the same time benefiting from the unique location of the church space.

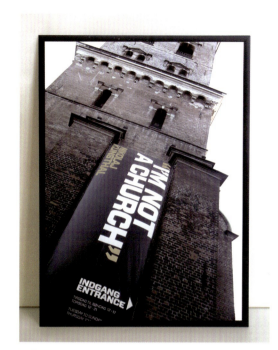

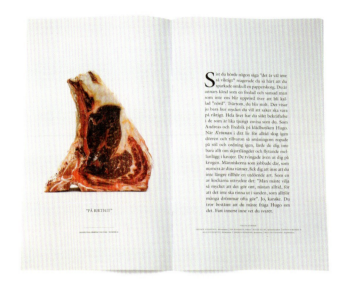
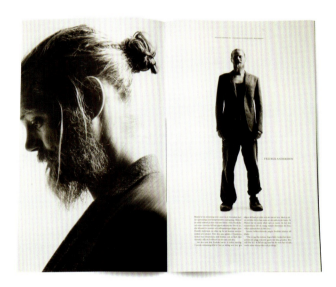

Hugo

Year of Completion_ 2012
Designer_ DRY Creative Projects
Photography_ DRY Creative Projects
Client_ Hugo

Hugo is an exclusive menswear shop in Stockholm with a long history and many regular customers. DRY Creative Projects has, among many other projects, created a packaging program, and a paper called "Friends of Hugo" that is published twice a year. People in the paper are regular customers of Hugo with interesting stories from work or private life.

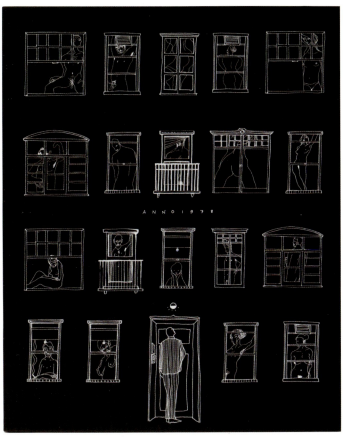

Moloobhoy & Brown

Year of Completion_ 2012
Design Firm_ Moloobhoy & Brown
Photography_ Moloobhoy & Brown
Client_ Moloobhoy & Brown

Moloobhoy & Brown's brand is a reflection of themselves and their principles. The "&" is the key to their collaborative approach with their clients, partners and suppliers. The paper stock and all materials were carefully chosen to give each item a tactile, timeless quality as well as a high production value. Moloobhoy & Brown's monogram embodies their partnership.

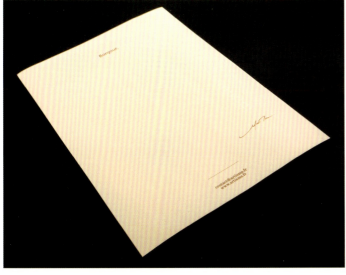
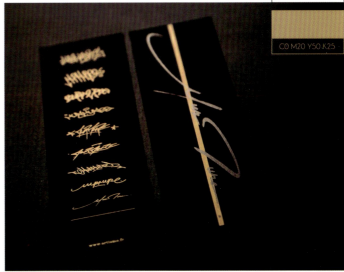

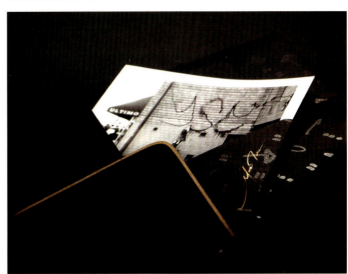

Artisme

Year of Completion_ 2012
Design Firm_ Murmure — Creative Agency
Photography_ Paul Ressencourt, Julien Alirol
Client_ Artisme

Defining their work as "artisme," this street-artists' co-op transfigures our urban spaces with drawings. Committed, dreamlike, or poetic, their projects skillfully interact with walls and their textures, papers, and drawings. Their desire is to be identified visually as elegant and mysterious, favoring image over information. The style consists of the creation of an artistic signature with urban influences.

Concrete Business Cards

Year of Completion_ 2012
Design Firm_ Murmure — Creative Agency
Photography_ Paul Ressencourt, Julien Alirol
Client_ Self Promotion

Playing with the notion of scales, Murmure created a set of business cards made of concrete. Using the smallest and most refined communication support enhanced this material, which is so characteristic of their environment. The refinement and the technique required for the typography highlight the harshness and the roughness of the material used.

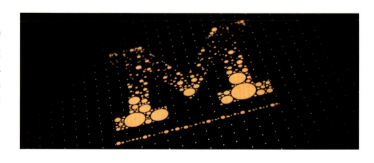

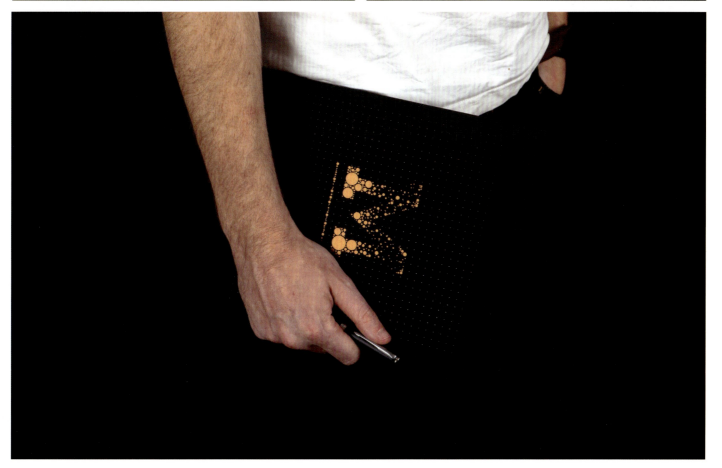

INDEX

+Quespacio
Location: Valencia, Spain
Tel: 963.303.156
Web: masquespacio.com

one Trick Pony
Location: Bellevue, USA
Tel: 609 704 2660
Fax: 646 619 4095
Web: www.1trickpony.com

Alan Crowne
Location: Sydney, Australia
Tel: +61 0 400 148 517
Web: www.alancrowne.com

Alex Matveev
Location: London, UK
Tel: +44 7944 014 814 376
Web: www.alexmatveev.co.uk

Alexandra Turban
Location: Nuremberg, Germany
Tel: 017634126241
Web: www.alexandraturban.de

Alicja Wydmanska
Location: Katowice, Poland
Tel: +48 693 819 750
Web: behance.net/rashell

Alphabetical
Location: London, UK
Tel: +44 020 3487 0690
Web: alphabeticalstudio.com

Alt Group
Location: Auckland, New Zealand
Tel: +64 9 360 3910
Web: www.altgroup.net

Ana Gomez Bernaus
Location: Los Angeles, USA
Tel: 9178556428
Web: www.anenocena.com

Analogue
Location: Leeds, UK
Tel: 0113 410330
Web: www.madebyanalogue.co.uk

Anoniwa
Location: Osaka, Japan
Tel: +81 (0)6 6961 0003
Fax: +81(0)6 7654 0976
Web: www.anoniwa.com

Apartment One
Location: New York, USA
Tel: 718 768 2191
Web: www.aptone.com

April Larivee
Location: Santa Ana, USA
Tel: 562 833 1957
Web: betweenhayandgrass.com

Arthography
Location: St. Petersburg, Russia
Tel: +7 812 309 56 80
Web: www.arthography.ru

Atipo
Location: Asturias, Spain.
Tel: 984190421
Web: www.atipo.es

Atipus
Location: Barcelona, Spain
Tel: +34 934851395
Web: www.atipus.com

Augusto Arduini & Giuditta Brusadelli
Add: Milan, Italy
Tel: 0039 347 3611910
Web: www.theclocksmiths.it

Berger & Föhr
Location: Boulder, USA
Tel: 303 588 1712; 720 323 7171
Web: bergerfohr.com

Botond Vörös
Location: Budapest, Hungary
Tel: +36 70 228 5187
Web: www.botondvoros.com

Brandoctor
Location: Zagreb, Croatia
Tel: + 385 1 6064 000
Fax: + 385 1 6192 599
Web: brandoctor.com

Bruketa&Žinić OM
Location: Zagreb, Croatia
Tel: +385 1 6064 000
Fax: +385 1 6064 001
Web: bruketa-zinic.com

Brunswicker Studio
Location: Copenhagen, Denmark
Tel: +45 4021 1033
Web: www.brunswicker.dk

Build
Location: London, UK
Tel: +44 0 20 8521 1040
Web: www.wearebuild.com

BüRO UFHO
Location: Singapore, Singapore
Tel: +65 98511145
Web: www.ufho.com

Catherine Renee Dimalla
Location: San Francisco, USA
Tel: 360 510 7793
Web: crdimalla.com

Chad Miller
Location: Newport, USA
Tel: 513-668-3172
Web: www.chdmlr.com

Cinking Studio
Location: Barcelona, Spain
Tel: +34 931 742 106
Web: www.cinkingstudio.com

COOEE
Location: Amsterdam, Netherlands
Tel: +31 618397297
Web: www.cooee.nl

Corn Studio
Location: Athens, Greece
Tel: +306947817393
Web: www.cornstudio.gr

Daniel Ting Chong
Location: Cape Town, South Africa
Tel: +27 82 69 12 056
Web: www.danieltingchong.com

Design Devision
Location: London, UK
Email: sayhello@designdevision.com
Web: www.designdevision.com

DRY Creative Projects
Location: Stockholm, Sweden
Tel: +46 8 21 88 00
Web: www.drycreativeprojects.com

Emanuele Cecini
Location: San Francisco, USA
Web: www.emanuelececini.com

Emil Karlsson
Location: Gothenburg, Sweden
Tel: +46 0739 227686
Web: www.ekpd.se

Farmgroup
Location: Bangkok, Thailand
Tel: +662 714 7278
Web: www.farmgroup.co.th

FEB Design
Location: Porto, Portugal
Tel: +351 226 008 525
Web: www.feb-design.com

Fettle
Location: Leeds, UK
Tel: +44 0113 8214 685
Web: www.fettledesign.com

FIBA Design
Location: Coimbra, Portugal
Tel: +351 239 403 185
Web: www.fibadesign.com

Flor Aguilar
Location: Wommelgem, Belgium
Tel: +32 0 3 295 88 57
Web: www.oraguilar.com

FRVR
Location: Prague, Czech Republic
Email: hi@frvr.cz
Web: frvr.cz

Gabriel Corchero Studio
Location: Madrid, Spain
Tel: +34 91 5060661
Web: www.gabrielcorchero.org

Gen Design Studio
Location: Braga, Portugal
Tel: +351 253 217 900
Web: www.gen.pt

Glad Creative
Location: Durham, UK
Tel: 0191 499 8390
Web: www.weareglad.com

Happy Creative Services
Location: Bangalore, India.
Tel: +080 41280225
Web: www.thinkhappy.biz

Higher
Location: Bratislava, Slovakia
Email: be@higher-uk.com
Web: www.higher-uk.com

Horizon Draftfcb
Location: Beirut, Lebanon
Tel: +961 1 387 600
Fax: +961 1 387 604
Web: www.draftfcb.com

Hyperakt
Location: New York, USA
Tel: (718) 855-4250
Web: hyperakt.com

ICK Studio
Location: Montevideo, Uruguay
Tel: +598 2900 3497
Web: ickstudio.com

Ineo Designlab
Location: Aarhus, Denmark
Tel: +45 8612 7062
Web: www.ineo.dk

Ingeborg Scheffers
Location: Amsterdam, Netherlands
Tel: +31 020 606 07 84
Web: www.ingeborgscheffers.nl

Jinah Lee
Location: Toronto, Canada
Tel: 647 882 7320
Web: www.jinahlees.com

John Barton
Location: London, UK
Email: info@johnbarton.co.uk
Web: www.johnbarton.co.uk

Katharinamauer.de
Location: Hamburg, Germany
Tel: +49 151 578 230 98
Web: www.katharinamauer.de

Lemongraphic
Location: Singapore, Singapore
Tel: +65 98224829
Web: www.lemongraphic.sg

lg2boutique
Location: Montreal, Canada
Tel: 514 281 8901
Web: lg2boutique.com

Livia Ritthaler
Location: London, UK
Email: hello@livia-ritthaler.de
Web: www.livia-ritthaler.de

Lundgren+Lindqvist
Add: Sockerbruket 17, Floor 06, SE-414 51
Gothenburg, Sweden
Tel: +46 31 757 11 00
Web: www.lundgrenlindqvist.se

Maibritt Lind Hansen
Location: Aarhus, Denmark
Tel: +45 3137 8244
Web: www.maibrittlindhansen.com

Maksim Arbuzov
Location: Moscow, Russia
Tel: +7 985 149 55 11
Web: www.maksimarbuzov.com

Marina Senabre Roca
Location: Valencia, Spain
Tel: 629 919 512
Web: www.labuhardi.com

Mark Kaiser
Location: Los Angeles, USA
Tel: 916 698 2756
Web: OmnibusDesign.com

Matadog Design
Location: Athens, Greece
Tel: +30 2109210061
Fax: +30 2109210061
Web: www.matadog.com

Mind Design
Location: London, UK
Tel: +44 020 7254 2114
Web: www.minddesign.co.uk

Moloobhoy & Brown
Location: Dubai, UAE
Tel: +971 04 458 6508
Fax: +971 04 458 6507
Web: www.moloobhoybrown.com

Murmure — Creative Agency
Location: Caen, France
Tel: +33 09 80 56 81 30
Web: www.murmure.me

Necon
Location: Wroclaw, Poland
Tel: + 48 605 331 691; + 48 71 718 85 85
Web: www.necon.pl

Noeeko
Location: Warszawa, Poland
Tel: +48 665 195 400
Web: www.noeeko.com

Núria Pujol Canals
Location: Barcelona, Spain
Email: nuriapujol@me.com
Web: www.nuriapujol.com

Pau Garcia Sanchez
Location: Barcelona, Spain
Tel: +34 628734187
Web: www.pauerr.com

Piotr Ploch
Location: Cracow, Poland
Tel: +48 793 912 929
Web: www.kreujemy.to

Piotr Steckiewicz
Location: Wroclaw, Poland
Tel: +48 791 842 838
Web: steckiewicz.prosite.com

Playoff Communication Agency
Location: Moscow, Russia
Tel: +7 495 532 6302
Web: playoffcs.ru

Solo
Location: Barcelona, Spain
Tel: +34 658 331 675
Web: www.solofficial.com

Somewhere Else
Location: Singapore, Singapore
Tel: +65 6297 7749
Web: www.somewhere-else.info

Sorbet Design
Location: Auckland, New Zealand
Tel: +64 9 4195665
Web: www.sorbetdesign.co.nz

Spring
Location: Vancouver, Canada
Tel: 604 683 0167
Web: www.springadvertising.com

Stefan Zimmermann
Location: Eschweiler, Germany
Email: kontakt@deszign.de
Web: www.deszign.de

Stefanie Horodko
Location: Detroit, USA
Email: stefanie.horodko@gmail.com
Web: www.pixelorperson.com

Studio Fnt
Location: Seoul, Korea
Tel: +82 2 337 0151
Fax: +82 2 337 5374
Web: www.studiofnt.com

Superbig Creative
Location: Seattle, USA
Tel: 206 767 3775
Fax: 212 656 1626
Web: www.superbigcreative.com

Teacake Design
Location: Manchester, UK
Tel: +44 (0)7834 483898; +44 (0)7811 327198
Web: teacakedesign.com

Thorbjørn Gudnason
Location: Copenhagen, Denmark
Tel: 45 28 30 29 15
Web: www.thorbjoerngudnason.com

Tiago Campeã
Location: Porto, Portugal
Email: mail@tiagocampea.com
Web: www.tiagocampea.com

Work in Progress
Location: Oslo, Norway
Tel: +47 92 09 45 73
Web: www.workinprogress.no

YR Studio
Location: Kediri, Indonesia
Tel: +62 877 590 490 79
Web: www.yr-studio.com

Coloring Your Brand

Author: Dopress Books
Commissioning Editors: Guo Guang, Mang Yu, Yvonne Zhao, Zhao Yiping
English Editors: Jenny Qiu, Vera Pan
Copy Editor: Frances Moxley Zinder
Book Designer: Peng Tao

©2013 by China Youth Press, Roaring Lion Media Co., Ltd. and CYP International Ltd. China Youth Press, Roaring Lion Media Co., Ltd. and CYP International Ltd. have all rights which have been granted to CYP International Ltd. to publish and distribute the English edition globally.

First published in the United Kingdom in 2013 by CYPI PRESS

Add: 79 College Road, Harrow Middlesex, HA1 1BD, UK
Tel: +44(0)20 3178 7279
E-mail: sales@cypi.net editor@cypi.net
Website: www.cypi.co.uk
ISBN: 978-1-908175-33-5

Printed in China